Henry Woodd Nevinson, John P Anderson

Life of Friedrich Schiller

Henry Woodd Nevinson, John P Anderson

Life of Friedrich Schiller

ISBN/EAN: 9783743377967

Manufactured in Europe, USA, Canada, Australia, Japa

Cover: Foto ©Thomas Meinert / pixelio.de

Manufactured and distributed by brebook publishing software (www.brebook.com)

Henry Woodd Nevinson, John P Anderson

Life of Friedrich Schiller

LIFE

OF

FRIEDRICH SCHILLER

BY

HENRY W. NEVINSON

LONDON
WALTER SCOTT, 24 WARWICK LANE
NEW YORK : THOMAS WHITTAKER
TORONTO : W. J. GAGE AND CO.
1889

All rights reserved.)

CONTENTS.

CHAPTER I.
                                                        PAGE

Schiller born at Marbach on the 10th of November, 1759; removal to Lorch and Ludwigsburg; the Court; early schooling; the military academy; a student of medicine; effect of military training; study of literature; youthful melancholy; the army doctor; personal appearance; early authorship; acting of the *Robbers*, 1782; flight . 11

CHAPTER II.

Difficulties at Mannheim; retreat at Bauerbach; playwright at Mannheim; mental characteristics of the period of "revolt;" the *Robbers;* plot; Karl Moor; style; causes of its success; *Fiesco;* its failure; *Plot and Passion;* the *Anthology* and other lyrics; influence of the early works; Schiller as a champion of liberty; French citizenship afterwards conferred on him as such; foundation of the *Thalia;* Körner's invitation; departure for Leipzig, 1785 24

CHAPTER III.

Hymn to Joy; change in Schiller; friendship with the Körners; life near Dresden; *Passion's Freethinking* and *Resignation; The Philosophic Letters;* empty speculations; *Don*

Carlos; the character and political significance of Posa; character of Philip, and ideal of a patriot king; hopes for human race; *The Artists;* first visit to Weimar, 1787; historical studies; beginning of the *Revolt of the Netherlands; The Ghostseer;* the Lengefeld family; Rudolstadt and the Saale; state of society there; Schiller at Volkstädt and Rudolstadt; *The Celebrated Woman; The Gods of Greece; The Artists;* appointment to a professorship at Jena, 1789 47

CHAPTER IV.

Jena; the University; first lecture; second course; betrothal; marriage, 1790; Schiller as historian; *Revolt of the Netherlands; The Thirty Years' War;* beginning of disease; the present from Denmark; study of Kant; powerful attraction of Kantism; Schiller's opposition to Kantian ethics, but belief in the Æsthetics; Schiller's æsthetic essays; *On Naïve and Reflective Poetry;* effect of Kantian philosophy on Schiller's art; visit to Suabia; death of the Duke of Würtemburg; return to Jena; end of Schiller's apprenticeship, 1794 74

CHAPTER V.

History of past intercourse with Goethe; Schiller's estimate of him after first interview; apparent jealousy; natural opposition; Goethe's low estimate of Schiller and his works; beginning of friendship; The Symbolic Plant; frequent intercourse and correspondence; effects on each; *The Hours;* causes of its failure; chaotic condition of German thought and literature; object of the

Xenia; their extraordinary effect, 1796; some examples of *Xenia;* other epigrams; increased productiveness; allegorical and philosophic poems; troubles in Suabia; death of Schiller's youngest sister and father; new house in Jena; the ballads, 1797; *Nadowessier's Dirge ;* Schiller's later ballads and lyrics; riddles in verse; return to drama; beginning of *Wallenstein,* 1798 98

CHAPTER VI.

The three divisions of *Wallenstein ;* why it cannot be called a triology; outline of *Wallenstein's Camp ;* the friar's sermon; temper of the army; *The Piccolomini ;* unimportance of this part of the play; the episode of Max and Thekla; characteristic creations of Schiller; *Wallenstein's Death;* account of the plot and the hero's character; effect of the play at the time; possible charge of weakness against Wallenstein's character; true value of the drama; visit of the King of Prussia; domestic troubles; *The Song of the Bell,* 1799; causes of its popularity; removal to Weimar; society there; national apathy and negligence . . . 129

CHAPTER VII.

Activity of Schiller's last years; *Maria Stuart,* 1800; growth of art displayed in it; sketch of plot; *The Maid of Orleans,* 1801; departure from historic truth; why to be regretted in this case; consequent failure of the central character; minor characters; Talbot's dying words; Schiller's reception in Leipzig; share in theatrical management; failure of attempts to raise public taste; Kotzebue's plot; removal to Esplanade; title of *von ; The Bride of Messina,* 1803; use of chorus; sketch of the plot;

visit of Madame de Staël; *William Tell*, 1804; Schiller's authorities; motives of the drama; use of scenery; character of Tell; scene of Gessler's death; anti-climax of the last act; visit to Berlin 156

CHAPTER VIII.

Last visit to Jena; renewed illness; translation of *Phèdre*; the *Homage of the Arts*; the drama of *Demetrius*; its foundation in Russian history; sketch of the plot; characters of Demetrius; contrasted with Mr. Browning's treatment of similar themes; character of Marina; and of Marfa; Schiller's renewed illness in the spring of 1805; his death on the 9th of May; Goethe's reception of the tidings; his *Epilogue* to the *Song of the Bell*; Schiller's character; his inborn horror of the mean and commonplace; his remoteness from the every-day world; his dislike of strangers; certain physical peculiarities of habit and manner; his general sanity of mind; his happy family life; his cheerful and sanguine temperament; strength of will inspired by hopefulness; effect of his enthusiasm on others; difficulties in estimating his position as a poet; the present time particularly unfavourable for such investigation; his service to his time perhaps greater than his permanent value; Goethe's comparison of Schiller and Byron; Schiller's services to German literature as an emancipator and a purifier 179

INDEX 199

BIBLIOGRAPHY.

LIFE OF SCHILLER.

CHAPTER I.

THE period of modern classical literature in Germany may almost be said to have begun in 1759, the year of Schiller's birth; for in that year appeared the *Letters on Literature*, in which Lessing criticised recent publications for the benefit of a friend who had been wounded at the beginning of the Seven Years' War, and delivered German poetry and letters from the false and artificial canons that had held sway since the time when the Thirty Years' War obliterated almost every genuine and national element in German thought. It may be noticed, also, that in the same year Rousseau was finishing the *Nouvelle Héloïse*, the influence of which on literature and popular sentiment was to be felt at least as fully in Germany as in France.

Like Goethe, who was ten years his senior, Schiller had the advantage of being born in South Germany, in one of the richest and sunniest of all the beautiful valleys that supply the main stream of the Rhine. His forefathers for some generations had lived in decent poverty, generally as bakers, in one or other of the

Suabian villages near Stuttgart; and his father had entered the service of the Duke of Würtemberg as army doctor, had been present in the Netherlands during the War of Austrian Succession, had taken the field again with the Würtemberg troops in the pay of France on the outbreak of the Seven Years' War, and had been a fugitive after their defeat at Leuthen. During the father's absence at the wars his wife remained in her parents' home, the Golden Lion at Marbach; and it was here that Friedrich Schiller, the poet, was born on the 10th of November 1759. The place stands on the Neckar, in the midst of gentle, vine-clad hills, a few miles down the stream from the capital, and is one of those ancient little towns whose walls and towers and high-pitched roofs, overhanging the crooked streets, still linger on in outlying districts of rural Germany, where nature has nothing to offer profitable enough for the manufacturer, nor melodramatic enough for the tourist.

At the end of the Seven Years' War, Schiller's father was able to return home, but he still held a small and ill-paid military appointment in the Duke's service; and soon afterwards the family were ordered to Lorch, a pleasant village on one of the Neckar's tributaries, some distance east of Stuttgart. The whole district is pervaded with reminiscences of Germany's early greatness. Waiblingen, the early home of Barbarossa's father, and the village from which the Ghibelline party took its name, stands on the same stream as Lorch; the hill of Hohenstaufen itself is close at hand, and in the ruined cloister by the village were the graves of the great Suabian dynasty. Besides a feeling for the romance of history, Schiller here imbibed his first regular instruction in letters from the kindly old parson of the place, whose influence and example naturally turned the boy's thoughts towards office in the Protestant church as his future profession. This inclination was readily encouraged by his parents, who were both simple-minded believers in Christianity, the mother having a tendency even to Pietism; whilst the father, who had dutifully stifled certain mutinous doubts, fulfilled the ritual incumbent on the head of an evangelical family with sober uprightness and military precision. Accordingly, when, at the end of 1766, the family removed to Ludwigsburg, in order that Captain Schiller might join a new regiment with some hope of regular pay, the boy was entered at the Grammar School there, from which he would advance in due course through a Cloister School to the Theological Faculty at some University.

But Ludwigsburg was hardly the place to encourage clerical aspirations. The reigning duke, Karl Eugen, of Würtemberg, had fixed his court there to spite the old capital of Stuttgart, where the Estates had ventured to protest against his method of offering his army for sale to the highest bidder, be it France or England, or even the Dutch colonies. In a few years he had converted the place into the envied model of all the petty princedoms in Germany, and succeeded in reaching a height of barbaric extravagance which the aristocratic mind regarded as evidence of the most advanced civilisation. Ludwigsburg was acknowledged to have approached most nearly, of all German capitals, to the splendour of Versailles. The new palaces, the gardens, parks, and lakes were the scene of revels in which the absurd side of the German nature was revealed by the wild struggle to be gay. Italian operas and French dances and pantomimes held the stage in the newly-erected theatres. For fifteen years the Italian composer, Jomelli, directed the music of the court. Year after year Vestris was hired at enormous cost to lead the dances for some months of the season. When the peace was concluded, and no power would make a fresh bid for the services of the army, the troops were retained on a war footing that they might swell the processions of shows and carnivals, and form picturesque backgrounds to military spectacles on the stage. Eight hundred useless horses were fed in the Duke's private stable. The forests were crammed with game; and the whole country was devastated that noble guests might slay at their ease, as the animals were driven past them on the great days of slaughter. Lakes were constructed on the tops of hills to be the scene of naval encounters, Venetian fêtes, and almost inconceivable devices of tasteless frivolity and ineptitude. Palace after palace arose, seven in all, within the space of a few years, often in the most remote and inconvenient situations. "Mon Repos" was built in the middle of a lake; the "Solitude" far away in the forest. Like most of his contemporaries, the Duke was carried away by a passion for the construction of those vast pseudo-classic piles that stud the face of Germany, and seem now to be pervaded by a peculiar melancholy. Nor were barbaric spectacles and debased architecture the only ducal passions. Since his wife had felt herself constrained to return to her mother, Wilhelmina, the famous sister of Frederick the Great, the Duke's profligacy had earned him distinction even among eighteenth-century princes. Gay Italian ladies swarmed in the Residenz, and in the houses of the nobility, nor did the Duke and his highborn friends despise the excitement of ravishing from their homes the daughters of respectable families in the neighbourhood. And to maintain the glories of this model German court, a thrifty and long-suffering people contributed their scanty pence, their honour, and their lives, year after year, with a bare protest and without the smallest hope of redress. No wonder we read that the life of the townspeople was corrupted by infection from the court, and that the few who kept themselves unspotted turned to Pietism as despair's last refuge in the midst of immorality and oppression.

During the six or seven years of Schiller's boyhood that were spent at Ludwigsburg, he inevitably received forcible impressions of the kind of life to which the highest and most civilised society in Germany aspired. But apart from the regular visits to the Italian Opera that were required by the Duke of all his officers and their families, the boy's own interest was mainly limited to the walls of his home and the Grammar School, where he was making fair progress. The family lived in retirement, the father devoting himself to the culture of trees, for which he obtained so high a reputation that it afterwards became his profession. It was during these years that Schiller first constructed German rhymes, mainly on religious subjects, the common themes of such German poets as he could then be acquainted with. His mother had brought him up on the quiet hymns and religious verses of Gellert and Utz, almost the only contemporary poets that had succeeded in reaching the hearts of the people, though it is true that the feeling for poetry was even then far more general among the lower and lower-middle classes in Germany than it has ever been in England. She herself had a genuine faculty for verse, and the father also was endowed with a certain literary instinct, for he wrote some successful treatises on his chosen horticultural pursuits, and could put his religious thoughts into rhyme when he had nothing better to do.

But just as Schiller was about to quit the Grammar School for the next step in clerical education, his quiet course of life, with its theological tendencies and harmless exercise in German or Latin verse, was rudely interrupted by the paternal consideration of the Duke for his subjects. For the last two or three years a remarkable change seemed to have been coming over the Duke's character. The amount of pleasure to be got out of the world is, after all, limited, and the Duke had reached the limit. Under the influence of a new and distinguished mistress, he was now entering upon a course of reformation that led him, at the age of fifty (1778), to issue a proclamation of repentance and promise of amendment to his loving subjects from every pulpit in his Dukedom. Sick of pleasure, he turned to philanthropy, the common resource of sickness. At his favourite palace of the "Solitude," in the forest west of Stuttgart, he established a Military Academy, originally designed for the orphans of officers, but afterwards extended into a general school for any promising children. A large girls' school on similar lines was also founded close by, and entrusted to the philanthrophic care of his amiable mistress, Franciska, Countess of Hohenheim, who acted as lady-superintendent and arbitress of morals to the establishment.

Pupils were obtained by various means; sometimes the advantages of free and sound education were bestowed on children whose fathers, as in the case of the poet Schubart, or the statesman Moser, were retained in prison year after year at the Duke's pleasure, untried, unaccused, and guilty only of a crime that would now be thought an honour. Sometimes, as in Schiller's case, the favour took the form of an offer which was equivalent to a command. As the Duke was determined to be philanthropic, it was obviously absurd that he should be thwarted for lack of subjects on whom to practise his good intentions.

Accordingly, in 1773, after a feeble effort at resistance, Schiller's father, who two years before had been appointed overseer of the "Solitude" gardens, was obliged to comply with the wishes of his benefactor, and sign the customary bond, making over his son to the Duke's service and command for the rest of his natural life, the choice of his future profession and appointment lying absolutely at the Duke's discretion. Schiller was sent for from Ludwigsburg, where he had remained as a boarder in a master's house since the removal of the family to the "Solitude," and was entered as a pupil of subordinate rank at the Military Academy, he being then nearly fourteen. He was set to study law, but after two years was allowed to change to medicine, since the Duke wanted students for that newly-instituted faculty. Five years careful training under Professor Abel, who some years later was to be one of Cuvier's earliest and most inspiring masters, gave Schiller considerable insight into medical science. A few relics of his studies have survived—analyses of post-mortem investigations and treatises on the dubious borderland between mental and physical laws, a favourite theme of speculation at the time; and in later life he sometimes thought of returning to the medical profession. But the bent of his mind was eminently unscientific; and even as a student he gained most distinction for perfunctory odes and exaggerated panegyrics on the virtues of the Duke and his mistress.

There were between three and four hundred pupils in the school, but they were sharply divided into two great classes, according to rank. In 1775 the institution was removed from the "Solitude" to Stuttgart, as a sign that the Duke's repentance was genuine, and that he was willing to receive his subjects back into favour. Schiller was thus shut out more than ever from his family circle. The strict discipline of a school, where every day was alike, and every daily event, even private prayer, went by word of command, was no doubt uncomfortable at the time; and the minute exactness of the etiquette was probably irritating, though to a boy formalism is natural. But, on the whole, these seven years of military training were of great service to Schiller. The school that within a few years could produce such men as Schiller, Dannecker the sculptor, and Cuvier, not to speak of over thirty others of whom we read that they rose to the highest positions in the German political world, cannot have been the stifling pit of tyranny which it is represented to have been by some writers on the subject. The teachers were men of high attainments and considerable sympathy. The Duke abandoned himself with devotion to his new passion for education; he seems to have been acquainted with the pupils individually, and to have watched their development, not wisely in every case, but at all events with care. Above all, we may attribute to the discipline itself that persistence, strength of will, and abhorrence of slovenliness in detail by which Schiller is honourably distinguished among his contemporaries. Except Lessing, to whom nature gave a temper of steel, no German writer of rank in that century did his work so cleanly. Unlike the rest, Schiller left few loose ends, and almost always had the grace to finish what he began.

At the Academy he passed from boyhood into youth, and his nature developed rapidly. He was early carried away by the tumultuous passion for literature. In literature all his other growing passions found their only food. Shakspeare he studied, though from him he turned away dissatisfied, his mind being then, and, indeed, throughout life, very far from Shakspearian. The works of indifferent poets, such as Klopstock and Gerstenberg, were devoured with enthusiasm; but it was Rousseau, Goethe, and Plutarch that changed and exalted the whole forces of his life. The flood of passionate and melancholy sentiment that had swept over the cultivated youth of Germany made its way at last through the jealous barriers of the Duke's Academy. Copies of the *Nouvelle Héloïse*, *Götz*, and, above all, *Werther*, were smuggled in and read in secret. Enthusiasm drove the students to imitation; it seemed so easy to reproduce what they felt so keenly. Schiller composed odes that were sometimes thought worthy of a place in the local papers. He tried his hand at a drama that was wisely destroyed, and before he was nineteen he had conceived the idea and completed some scenes of the *Robbers*.

Literature possessed him, and to gain time for writing, he would retire to the hospital on sick leave. Even at his work copies of the poets surreptitiously took the place of physical text-books. As was natural, he sank into despondent gloom, just at that time more than usually characteristic of youth. The world had turned black. He longed for death, and the thought of suicide was continually before him. There was probably something unreal and theatrical in all this. Gloom and suicide were in fashion. But imagined misery is in youth as intense, or at least as obtrusive, as any real misery that comes after. A curious record of these years has come down to us in the shape of a medical report by Schiller himself on a case which the fatherly Duke had entrusted to his special care. The patient was "hypochondriacal," had lost faith in everything in heaven and earth except the Duke's kindness, and was with the greatest difficulty restrained from suicide, for which he entreated Schiller to give him the needful drug. The accuracy with which Schiller traces the inner workings of the poor creature's mind may be taken to prove personal knowledge of the disease; but at the same time, as he suggests practical remedies, and is as rational as an alderman in attributing the disorder to derangement of the stomach, we may suppose that with himself the crisis was already over.

This was in the summer of 1780, when his deliverance from the Academy was close at hand. At the end of the previous year he had for the first time seen Goethe, who visited the school with Karl August of Weimar on their return from Switzerland. Having recited a satisfactory medical thesis before the Duke in November 1780,

Schiller was appointed one of the army surgeons in Stuttgart with a salary of about £20 a-year. Cramped in the old-fashioned Prussian uniform, a little cap on his head, his hair arranged in three crisp little powdered curls on each side, and a long pig-tail at his back, almost throttled by a tight horse-hair stock, his gaiters padded out till they were thicker than his thighs, he is represented to us as moving stiffly about like a stork. In figure he was fairly tall, but very slim. His head projected from his shoulders, partly owing to shortness of sight. He was pale, but much given to blushing, especially under the excitement of talking. His hair was deep red, and in later years was worn long and flowing. The forehead was high and singularly full above the temples. The eyebrows almost met at the base of the large and strongly-hooked nose, and were continually contracted into a thoughtful frown. The eyes, of a dark, uncertain colour, were set deep under the brows, and generally looked dreamy rather than inspired. The whole face expressed loftiness, intensity, and strength of will, at all events in maturity; and these characteristics were fully borne out by the high cheekbones, the long, thin mouth, the under lip slightly projecting, and the massive chin that seemed to hang forward from the throat. In later years the look of intensity was perhaps heightened by the prolonged agony of fatal disease. The voice was harsh and unpleasant, but he talked well, though with great rapidity.

In the comparative freedom of his new mode of life, Schiller continued his literary pursuits with increased energy. He wrote for various journals, and even conducted a critical quarterly, called a *Repertorium*, through three numbers of existence. He collected his own odes and lyrics, and with contributions from kindred versifiers formed them into an *Anthology* for 1782. Above all, he completed the *Robbers*, and had it printed at his own charges in July 1781. This gained him local distinction at once, and he already found himself almost famous when Dalberg, the director of the Mannheim theatre, undertook to produce a revised version of the piece, the scene being, for safety's sake, put back from the eighteenth century to the sixteenth. It was performed for the first time on January 13th, 1782, to a house that was crowded by all the light and culture of the neighbouring cities. Iffland, afterwards the famous actor and director in Berlin, then in his twenty-third year, took the part of the villain, and made a great impression. The whole play aroused extraordinary enthusiasm. Schiller was present, and was rapturously received. In the summer of the same year he paid another stolen visit to Mannheim to witness a fresh performance; but on his return the Duke got wind of it, and Schiller suffered a fortnight's arrest for breach of discipline. This was followed by a worse blow still. The Swiss canton of the Grisons complained to the Duke that the author of the *Robbers* had insulted their nation by calling it the modern Athens of scoundrels. The Duke felt he had been patient long enough, and Schiller was peremptorily ordered never to write another word. With the wild plaudits of crowded theatres still ringing in his ear, this was too much for a human poet's endurance. The fate of Schubart warned him that he might as well die at once as disobey. Flight alone remained. He made one last visit to the family circle in the "Solitude;" took a tearful farewell of his mother; and, while Stuttgart was in a tumult of illumination at the arrival of certain Russian notabilities, he stole away one September evening, 1782, accompanied by a young musician, who was his devoted admirer. They drove northwards to Mannheim, outside the Würtemberg territory, and escaped.

There seems to have been little serious attempt at pursuit, though for many months Schiller thought it necessary to live the life of a hare. He seldom saw his parents and three sisters again, but always continued to correspond with them, especially with his elder sister, Christophine. It is to the Duke's credit that he did not visit the sin of the child upon the father. The upright old man held his honourable position at the "Solitude" till his death during the troubles of 1796.

CHAPTER II.

CUT adrift from home and the associations and supports of his youth, Schiller was now to be exposed to nearly all the miseries of the slighted poet's lot. In Mannheim the theatrical authorities did not venture to welcome a refugee, and were probably afraid that he and his plays would become a troublesome acquisition. Driven by fear, he journeyed to Frankfurt on foot with his unselfish musical friend.* Driven by hunger, they returned to a hiding-place in the village of Oggersheim, near Mannheim, and there remained for a time, hoping vainly that a new play might be accepted by Dalberg, or that money might be raised on poems, or even supplied from home. At last, as disappointment followed disappointment, and apprehension and poverty deepened every day, he wrote in despair to a lady whose name deserves to be remembered among the patrons of letters. Frau von Wolzogen, a widow of good family and moderate means, had been living at Stuttgart for the education of her children, and through

* His name was Streicher; he afterwards attained some celebrity in Vienna, and died there in 1833.

them had become acquainted with Schiller before his flight. Guided by her insight into talent, or more probably by mere woman's kindness, she now offered him her country-house at Bauerbach, near Meiningen, as a harbour of refuge, and advanced him sums of money from time to time, expectation of repayment being perhaps a higher testimony to her power of faith than even her confidence in his genius. In December 1782, Schiller retired for eight months to the quiet homestead on the southern fringe of the great Thuringian forest, with the northern slopes of which he was in after life to be so closely connected. He spent the time in working out the two dramas, *Fiesco* and *Plot and Passion*, both of which were already well advanced before he left Mannheim, and in vaguely perusing miscellaneous literature from the Meiningen library. Here he became acquainted with the learned and melancholy librarian, Reinwald, who afterwards married his sister Caroline—unfortunately for her. It was an interval of peace, and naturally was occupied with day-dreams of love. For Schiller was very "inflammable," and, in youth, was perhaps even unusually inconstant. His benefactress, however, though willing to give him shelter and advance him money, regarded the security of genius as insufficient for a daughter's happiness; at all events, in July 1783, it was thought best that he should go back to Mannheim for a time to look after his plays and other interests, and he never returned. In Mannheim he received an appointment as playwright to the theatre, out of which, with good-luck, he might hope to make £50 a-year, or rather more. But the engagement only lasted for one year after all, and in August 1784 Schiller was adrift again, more grievously in debt, more desperate of the future. His two new dramas, *Fiesco* and *Plot and Passion*, had, however, been produced in the winter and spring of that year; and as the next few months after his retirement from the theatre mark a fairly distinct crisis and turning-point in his history, we may pause here to consider the general character of these earlier works.

A lion rampant with the motto, "*In Tyrannos*," was engraved as the frontispiece to the printed copies of the *Robbers*, and the collection of lyrics called an *Anthology* was expressly dedicated "To Death, my Lord and Master." The phrases were significant. Revolt and gloom are the two leading notes of almost everything that Schiller wrote in his youth. It was a time when the German mind was still seething in chaotic confusion from the effect of Herder's early criticism, and of such a masterpiece of passionate description and analysis as *Werther*. The spirit of revolt took many forms—almost every form but the political. It was ready to attack all moral and literary laws and restraints, to throw off all the conventions of society, to sweep away all the innocent frippery of manners, to involve distinctions of rank, the marriage-laws, and the recognised costume in the same destruction. It was a "return to nature," an attempt to shake off the oppression of a false civilisation. But at present, for Schiller and the other earlier leaders of the movement, the struggle for freedom was accompanied by little sense of exhilaration, for it seemed to be of but little avail. The apostles of freedom and passion were, after all, few and youthful; with age most people become the willing victims of moral and speculative restraints, and cease to trouble about first principles; and German formality has always been very tough. The temper of those years of "Storm and Stress" was consequently characterised, for the most part, by yearning melancholy and regretful gloom. It would be a mistake, however, to identify this uneasy dissatisfaction with pessimism. Youth had then no doubts as to the possibility and power of its ideals. Belief in the efficacy of profound passion, disinterested virtue, and magnanimity on the heroic scale was very genuine; there was no touch of cynicism in the movement; it was desperately in earnest, and in this perhaps it differed most from its later Byronic development. Only the mind, oppressed by the hard realities of a society where love was frivolous, virtue calculating, and intellect uninspired, gloomily recognised that its struggles for expansion were as yet but labour lost. To a spirit which, reversing the old Greek doctrine, could hardly believe excess to be even possible, the limits of eighteenth-century existence were indeed narrow. It seemed to beat in vain against the walls of its prison-house, and suicide was the last protest of its despair. So far as it will be remembered in the history of thought, the literature of this movement of revolt, this sudden and bewildering reappearance of the deep under-current of human passion, may be said to have begun in Germany with *Werther*, and to have ended with the three early plays of Schiller.

In the *Robbers*, which made far the deepest impression of the three, though as a work of art it is inferior to *Plot and Passion*, we have heroic revolt against the limitations of everyday morality. It is an appeal for grandeur of action, even though such action should override not only the maxims of albums and utilitarian philosophies, but the very laws that are said to form "the bulwarks of society." We might almost say that there are two heroes in the story, for Franz Moor, the villain of the piece, is raised to something like sublimity by excess of wickedness, and it may be noticed that his part was always considered the most striking on the stage, and was entrusted to the best actor. The plot is very slight, and abounds in obvious absurdities. It is the story of Gloucester and his two sons over again. Franz Moor, who is evidently modelled on Edmund, poisons his tearful old father's mind against the elder brother Karl by forged letters and false reports. Having by such stratagems secured the succession to the inheritance, he next turns over in his mind various devices for putting his father out of the way as soon as possible, and, in order to try the effect of a sudden shock, he suborns one of his creatures to bring false news of Karl's death at the battle of Prague. By this means he also hoped to supplant his brother in the affections of Amalia, one of those feeble and sentimental creatures, all tears and sighs and raving moonshine, that have so often done duty for heroines in German literature and life. The fraud is only partially successful. The childish old father, it is true, faints at the news, and is borne off for dead; Franz enters upon the estates with shameless threats against his new tenants; but Amalia resists his violent approaches, and remains overwhelmed in unbroken woe, only longing for death that she may dream of her Karl till the resurrection arouse her to the heaven of his embrace.

Meantime, in an earlier scene, Karl has been

discovered in the midst of wild young comrades characteristically perusing Plutarch, from the contemplation of whose heroes he has learned to loathe his own petty age of critics, professors, and commentators. He longs for action in the grand style. He chafes against the laws. "Law," he cries, "has never yet produced a man of true grandeur. It is freedom that hatches the colossal and the extreme. O that the spirit of Hermann still glowed in the ashes! Set me at the head of a band of fellows like myself, and in Germany a republic would arise, compared to which Rome and Sparta would seem like nunneries." Whilst he is in this ambitious mood a letter from Franz is brought, falsely announcing that his father has cast him off, and ceased to regard him as a son. Karl's rage is stupendous. He involves the whole human race in his curses. He would poison the sea, and end at once the whole generation of ungrateful man. Grasping at a comrade's suggestion, he rapidly organises his friends into a faithful band of brigands, under his own leadership. "My soul thirsts for action," he wildly cries, "my spirit for freedom." With murder and theft he will trample law under his feet, and avenge his lacerated feelings on humanity at large. He exchanges a kind of coronation oath with his followers; and full of the lust of slaughter and joyful expectation of their latter end, they all troop off to the Bohemian forest, which they have selected as the most suitable stage for their prowess.

In the forest Karl becomes a king of men indeed. He showers plundered gold; he bathes his horse in wine; his fingers are thick with rings torn from the oppressor. The band of eighty followers pursue their trade with unequalled valour and atrocity. They rob and murder, and storm cities, and violate nunneries with an energy that in time attracts the attention of the police. Devoted to their captain, they refuse to surrender him, though surrounded by troops and tempted by the greatest rewards. With Karl at their head they fight their way out. Three hundred of the foemen fall for the loss of one. But Karl, through all scenes of plunder and bloodshed, retains a magnanimity that separates him from the common herd. He has no care for booty. Like a modern Socialist, he, despoils the rich mainly for their own good. After all, his motives are almost philanthropic. He feeds the orphan and relieves the oppressed. His bloodiest enterprise is for the rescue of a condemned comrade. Soft memories, sweet impulses of a fading innocence, still melt his heart with yearning and regret. He weeps over the setting sun; he calls to mind the days when he could not sleep if he had forgotten his evening prayer. The beauty of the world fills him with unutterable woe. He hungers for happiness and is haunted by an ideal of unattainable perfection. Eternity fills his thoughts, and he meditates solving the ultimate problems of existence by suicide. What though he should spend eternity in analysing the confused picture of universal woe? What though birth after birth should but remove him from one stage of misery to another? Even death cannot deprive him of the freedom to die. In the midst of such high and melancholy thoughts he very naturally shudders to reflect that fate had made of him a brazen bull, "in whose glowing belly mankind is set to roast;" and in the end he is forced to cry, "With wailing and gnashing of teeth I discover that two such men as I would shatter the whole fabric of the moral world." If "magnificence in sin" was his object, he ought certainly to have been satisfied.

But he cannot forget his love, and driven by love, he ventures in the disguise of a northern Count to visit the castle where now his brother is supreme, and Amalia sits imprisoned like a captive bird. Amalia has not the wit to recognise the stranger, though with some dismay she finds herself rapidly becoming unfaithful to the memory of the exiled Karl; but Franz sees through his disguise clearly enough to arrange for his murder, and the danger is only averted by the fidelity of an old servant. The episode ends ineffectively, having only given opportunity for some touching reminiscences of childhood, and some interviews between the lovers, in which the main interest lies in wondering how much strain the heroine's stupidity will bear. The next scene opens with the song of the Robbers, still sung in the body of the theatre by Jena students when the play is performed at Weimar year by year. After the song, the robbers fall to quarrelling and murdering amongst themselves till they are interrupted by Karl's return. Gradually they drop asleep in a circle round him, and he is left singing of the meeting of Cæsar and Brutus on the banks of Styx, and meditating till far into the night on time and fate and death. As midnight strikes, someone comes through the wood, and approaches the ruined castle by which the robbers are encamped. It is Hermann, the creature whom Franz had used as a false messenger, and for other purposes of his own. Unconscious of the presence of Karl and the Robbers, he speaks:—

"*Hermann.* Hark, hark! How the screech-owl cries. There's twelve o'clock striking in the village. Good. Now knavery sleeps. In this desert there is none to listen. [*He advances to the castle, and knocks.*] Arise, thou man of sorrows, that dwellest in this tower! Thy supper is ready.

Karl [*drawing back softly*]. What may this mean?

A Voice [*from the castle*]. Who knocks? Ha? Is it you, Hermann, my raven?

Hermann. Yes, it is Hermann, thy raven. Climb up to the grating and eat. [*Owls cry.*] Drearily sing the partners of thy sleep, old man. Is it good? [*pointing to the food.*]

The Voice. I'm so hungry. Thanks to Thee, who sendest ravens, for bread in the wilderness. And how is my dear child, Hermann?

Hermann. Hush! Listen! A sound like people breathing! Don't you hear something?

The Voice. What? Do you hear anything?

Hermann. Only the sighing of the wind through the crevices of the tower, a music that makes one's teeth chatter and one's nails turn blue. Hark! There it is again! I seem to hear a kind of breathing all the time. You've someone with you, old man.

The Voice. Do you see anything?

Hermann. Farewell, farewell. This place is haunted. Back with you to your hole. He that must help and avenge you is above. O, accursed son!"

As he is hastening away, Karl seizes him, but he escapes whilst Karl is breaking through the grating with a burglar's skill. From the depths of the tower there emerges an old man, emaciated to a skeleton. "Pity on a wretched creature! Pity!" he pleads. "That is my father's voice," cries Karl, starting back. This is the dramatic crisis of the play.

> "Schiller! that hour I would have wished to die,
> If through the shuddering midnight I had sent
> From the dark dungeon of the tower time-rent
> That fearful voice, a famished Father's cry—
> Lest in some after moment aught more mean
> Might stamp me mortal!"*

The whole horrible story is soon unfolded. The old man had revived from his fainting-fit at the false news of Karl's death, to find himself shut in a coffin ready for burial. He scratched on the lid. It was opened by his son Franz, who shut it down again with the remark: "What! are you going to live forever?" and had then conveyed the coffin to the deserted tower with Hermann's aid, and sunk his father into a foul dungeon to starve. Wild with fury, Karl calls up his robber-band, and commands them to seize his old home, and bring Franz before him alive.

An hour or two later in the same night, Franz is discovered uneasily wandering about the corridors of his castle, haunted by ghostly alarms and terrible dreams of the Judgment Day and his own damnation. He sends for the parson, in order that sceptical disputation may relieve his feelings; but the parson turns on him with unchristian triumph, and by taunts and threats goes far to shake his disbelief in God and immortality. Hardly is he alone again when he hears the shouting of the robbers as they pour in upon the castle. In an agony of

---

* Coleridge's *Sonnet to the Author of* "*The Robbers.*"

terror he entreats his trembling servants to pray for him. He himself pours out the rather ambiguous prayer: "Hear me, God, in heaven! It is the first time I have ever prayed, and be sure I will never do it again. Hear me, God, in heaven! I have been no common murderer; I have not wasted my powers on trifles, O Lord!" The castle is on fire. Deserted by his followers, Franz listens to the flames, as they rush nearer, and to the shouts of the coming foe. They beat at the door. It cracks, and falls in. As it falls, he strangles himself with the golden strings of his hat.* The Robber, who had vowed to take him alive, shoots himself. When the news of his brother's death is brought, Karl is conversing with his old father, who does not yet recognise him. Amalia is then led in by another division of the band. There is general recognition, and at the thought that his Karl is a captain of brigands and cut-throats, the old man dies in earnest without a word. The lovers' brief dream of an ecstatic future is cut short by the more prosaic Robbers, who claim Karl for their own, and remind him of his oath never to leave them. In despair, Amalia asks for death, and Karl kills her himself, for "Moor's beloved must only die by Moor's own hand." He then resigns his position as leader, and amidst the sneers of the company goes to surrender himself into the hands of justice. Magnanimous and philanthropic, a true disciple of Rousseau to the last, he bethinks him of a poor labourer who has eleven children, and can now be enriched for life by the reward offered for his capture.

* In the revised version, he leaps into the flames—a more dignified exit.

It is difficult for a modern Englishman to read even the bare plot of such a school-boy production without a sense of burlesque. And the style is perhaps even more outrageous than the plot. It is written in the roughest prose, and abounds in Suabian Billingsgate. The stage is drowned with tears and blood, and the air cleft with ravings. The heroine spits, and slaps, and chases the villain about the stage with a dagger. Every feeling and motive is exaggerated to absurdity. There is no relief, no shade, no dramatic complexity of character. The critics at the time were not slow in demonstrating faults so obvious. The success of the play was held up as a proof of the miserable and uneducated taste of the vulgar. Together with all Schiller's early works, it was treated with abusive scorn by the critical press of Berlin. Goethe, finding it still the rage on his return from Italy, was driven to despair of his country. Schiller himself pointed out its weaknesses in an excellent critique published soon after the production of the play. And yet its success was indubitable. Perhaps no literary work of the last century, except *Werther*, made so profound an impression on the German mind; and what is more strange is that it has continued to hold the stage, perhaps more successfully than any other German drama, especially in the neighbourhood of university towns. Remembering that it had been the fashion to compare poor old Frau Karsch to Sappho, and Klopstock to Milton, we may pass over the frequent contemporary comparison of Schiller to Shakespeare with a smile. But even the hostile critics were obliged to admit that no piece had created such a sensation. Karl Moor was welcomed with the same kind of enthusiasm with which our grandfathers welcomed the Corsair. Boys conspired to enact the Robbers in real life. There was some apprehension that the fashion for suicide would now give way to a fashion for murder, far more embarrassing to general society. The heart of the nation was profoundly moved, in spite of the opposition of critics and the coldness of the upper classes. A prince once said to Goethe: "If I had been God on the point of creating the world, and had foreseen that Schiller would write the *Robbers* in it, I should not have created it." A French observer noticed that, as a rule, the nobility were not present at the representations, and that it was the common people that filled the theatre with applause. The brooding spirit of dissatisfaction and revolt had found a voice; and there was in the *Robbers* an appeal to the deeper nature of man, to the grander impulses of youth, an appeal that seldom fails when a sceptical and artificial age is breaking-up of its own aridity.

Schiller's next dramatic work, *The Conspiracy of Fiesco in Genoa*, though free from many of the absurdities of the *Robbers*, did not arouse the same excitement. On the whole, it was deservedly a failure. The theme was suggested by a passage in Rousseau, where Fiesco is compared to the heroes of Plutarch; and the motive is the revolt of republican virtue against tyranny. Schiller himself attributed the comparative ill-success of the play, perhaps truly, to the German want of free political feeling. Though the scene is laid in the Genoa of the middle of the sixteenth century, the description of the court and society, of the brutality and lust of the younger tyrant, Gianettino Doria, and of his shameless sister,

SCHILLER. 37

Julia, is obviously German, being drawn, in fact, from Schiller's own too intimate acquaintance with court life. But there was little sign in Germany of the active republican spirit that placed Fiesco at the head of a conspiracy which shook the Dorias from their throne, and afterwards, with many regrets over human fate, drowned its leader lest he should become a tyrant in turn. The German passion for constitutional liberty was mainly theoretic and convivial. The childlike admiration for princes as such was still so profound that it even now survives after a century of democratic crazes. But apart from political motive, the play had not strength in itself to ensure success. The action is uncertain, and is interrupted by episodes. A crowd of insignificant figures distract the interest. The heroine, Fiesco's wife, is as unreal as Amalia, and even more ineffectual. What is worse, the character of Fiesco himself is indistinctly drawn, and fails to arouse enthusiasm. In the middle of the play also he sacrifices what little sympathy the audience might have otherwise felt in his fate. For by a heartless stratagem he drives the erring Julia to own her passion on her knees before him, and then, in the moment of her shame and surrender, reveals her to his wife, who all the time has been purposely hidden behind the hangings, as a witness to the triumph of his coldly philosophic virtue.

Schiller has, of course, not hesitated to adapt history to the exigencies of drama. The drowning of the historical Fiesco, for instance, was entirely accidental; but Schiller was right in maintaining that in drama pure accident should have no part. It seems, therefore, all the more strange that what is, after all, the central and most striking scene in the play—the death of Leonore—should depend solely upon accident. On the night of the conspiracy she goes raving out into the street in her ecstatic way, determined to act Portia to Fiesco's Brutus, arms herself with the weapons of the first corpse she trips upon—it happens to be the body of Gianettino—encounters her husband, and is slain by him in mistake. He discovers the error at the moment of triumph, whilst the people and his fellow-conspirators are hailing him Duke of Genoa. The situation is pathetic, but is none the less as accidental and devoid of motive as may be.

But any damage that Schiller's reputation may have suffered from the failure of *Fiesco* was amply retrieved by the success of *Plot and Passion* (*Kabale und Liebe*), a play that set the chord of popular emotion vibrating at once, and, as a theatrical piece, has remained one of the most welcome of all Schiller's dramas. The Berlin critics, it is true, denounced it as a " disgrace to the age," but the fact was that the critics, like most men of learning, had lost touch of the age, and only became more abusive the further the great movements of the time swept past them. The general idea of the plot was no doubt suggested by reminiscences of many a similar incident in the scandalous history of the Würtemberg court, and the same theme of *mésalliance* had been used in comedy by Diderot and a German playwright. The worldly old President of some intriguing little German court, in order to preserve for himself a position won, in the first instance, by dishonourable and criminal means, determines that his son Ferdinand shall marry the mistress of the reigning prince. She is an Englishwoman of high family, and, in spite of her compromising

SCHILLER.

position, is possessed of every virtue. She has, besides, herself conceived a pure and ardent affection for Ferdinand. But the course of this promising arrangement is crossed by the perversity of the young man, who has formed a passionate and, what is worse, an honourable attachment to Louise, the daughter of old Miller, the fiddler. The situation is worked out with skilful pathos, and introduces vivid pictures of barbarous aristocratic society. We hear how the prince makes noble amends to the woman he has ruined by a superb wedding-present of diamonds, for the purchase of which seven thousand of his subjects have been driven from their homes into exile, whilst those who protested were shot. We see the courtiers devoting all the energies of life to intrigues and counterplots for offices not worth the holding, and employing all the subtleties of diplomacy to avenge the loss of a little hair-powder, or dispute the honour of picking up a garter. We see the honest old fiddler and his wife hurried off to prison at the President's word, whilst their daughter is charged as a wanton. Violence failing, the President and his accomplices adopt the stratagem of forcing Louise, by threats against her father's life, to write a compromising letter making an assignation with one of them. The letter is, of course, put in Ferdinand's way. By the terms of her oath she is compelled to admit guilt. In vain she visits the Lady Milford in her palace, and induces her, by the power of sheer innocence, to renounce Ferdinand and devote herself to unimpeachable virtue for the future. Louise's reputation is stained, and for her lover existence becomes impossible. He comes to see her for the last time, and again she dares not deny his charges. With idyllic simplicity he asks for lemonade, and secretly drops poison into it. Both drink, and as they die he receives the confession of her purity. His father, the President, enters in time to listen to the last reproaches of a younger generation in whom an ideal of love had arisen, different in kind from the amorous frivolity of courts—the only love intelligible to him. Thus the revolt of passion against the stiff worldliness of civilised existence finds for itself, under defeat, its most dignified consummation. As in the other two plays, the end is full of desperation and gloom. The world was still too strong, the bonds of society too tightly clamped.

The same spirit of dissatisfaction and gloomy revolt against the limitations imposed by life on the exaggerated aspirations and passions of youth pervades the greater number of the lyrics contributed by Schiller to the *Anthology* or published in other forms during these years. Selections made from them at a later time now appear in the ordinary editions of Schiller's works as *Poems of the First Period*. For the most part they deal with themes of death and the grave, of melancholy regret for the flight of beauty, of lamentation over joys that the heart conceives but can never attain, or passionate yearnings that will not be stilled. The poet would peer into the secrets of space and eternity; he dreams he wanders through the infinite ways of the universe; he catches glimpses of the pale realms of death, and hears the long sigh of lost souls in Tartarus as "they ask each other in anxious whisper whether the end be not yet come." Like Shelley in his early poems, he feels an irresistible attraction to the grave and all the hateful symbolism of decay. He cannot keep out the devouring worm even from his love lyrics. The poems "To Laura" were, no doubt, inspired, like most young poets' work, by an ideal of womanhood in general rather than by one particular object of love ; but if, as is said, they were dedicated to an easy going young widow who was his landlady in Stuttgart, we may wonder with what feelings she received her poet's assurances that he already seemed to see her eye growing dim, her roses fading, her cheek furrowed with the storms of age, till at last her beauty should return to the region of night and to the dust of which it was made.

But in the midst of much that is merely emotional, vague, and uncertain, two poems, at least, stand out with the advantage of distinctness in the general gloom. *The Infanticide* is the long lamentation of a deserted girl who has murdered her love-child, and is now brought to the scaffold. The death-bell sounds ; she takes farewell of the world and the joys of her childhood. She thinks with a pang that at this moment her betrayer may be deceiving another. She remembers her child, the innocent reproaches of its face, the dumb, unanswerable questionings of its existence that drove her to desperation. She calls for curses on her lover, and prays that the baby's ghost may haunt him in this world and the next. In the same breath she forgives him, and with a warning to others endowed with beauty's curse, yields herself up to death. Nothing could be more undramatic, nothing more unlike the words and thoughts that such a woman would express at such a moment. But by the mere power of its appeal, by the pathos of the situation, so common and so tragic continually, by a certain wealth and magnificence of language that characterise most of Schiller's work even from the first, though in reality rather allied to rhetoric than poetry, the poem struck the popular imagination at once, and has remained one of the most familiar of Schiller's lyrics. It is said, indeed, that every nurse-maid in Germany knows it by heart; but this, of course, may be due rather to the attractiveness of the subject than to the poet's art. The other most distinctive poem of the collection is very different in subject and treatment. It is called *The Battle*, and is a vivid and realistic picture, in irregular and mostly unrhymed metre, of one of those numerous encounters which Schiller must have heard described by his father over and over again in his boyhood. Like a thunder-cloud the army rolls up to the field. The command passes down the ranks, and the troops stand in silence waiting. Suddenly the enemy's flags and bayonets are seen, bright with the morning sun. The firing begins; the armies are locked in deadly embrace; many fall:

> " High spurts the blood at the throat,
> The living take the place of the dead, the foot
> Stumbles over the corpses—
> 'You too, Franz?' 'Take my love to Lottie, my lad!'
> Still wilder rages the strife.
> 'That I will '—O God ! my comrades, look there !
> How the grape-shot bursts behind us !—
> 'I'll take your love to Lottie, my lad !
> Sleep soft ! Where bullets rain thickest,
> I rush in desperation on.'"

If we try to discover wherein the value of Schiller's early works really lay, what was the secret of their influence— for, as often happens in the case of poets, these immature productions exercised more immediate influence on contemporary thought than the more finished and artistic works of his manhood—we shall perhaps find it in the increased demand they make on the great passions that are the mainsprings of human action. Compare *Plot and Passion* with Lessing's *Miss Sara Samson*, which was probably the best play of that kind then holding the stage. Both are tragedies of modern life; both deal with the theme of love crossed by the dictates of society. But what a difference in the tone, in the very meaning of the word love! It seems as though we had passed into a different world, so greatly is the tragedy deepened and strengthened by pure intensity of passion, under the stress of which the standards and sanctions, long consecrated by the usage of a polite civilisation, suddenly vanish, to make room for grander laws. Something elemental has reappeared in these works, something that takes us back to the primal forces of nature. Nor was it surprising that the reappearance should be accompanied by an outburst of savage absurdity. The rhetorical satire that too often takes the place of poetry, the doubtful humour, the coarseness and barbarisms that defile or render ridiculous so much of Schiller's early productions, are but the rude and awkward struggles of the new-born modern spirit. They may be called the literary September-massacres of the German Revolution. We seem to be watching the stormy dawn of a new period of rapid and passionate expansion, a period that has not yet drawn to its close. A new movement was astir, a movement that was to criticise every conclusion and question every formula. The origin of this new spirit was passionate and gloomy, and again at a later period of its growth it was to find its highest moral sanction in depth of passion, and its philosophy in gloom. Nevertheless, it has been throughout a spirit of growth, of high demands on life, and of self-development. It has, in short, been the spirit of liberty.

And it was due to the *Robbers*, and these other early plays, that Schiller was first recognised as an apostle of liberty and revolt even outside the boundaries of Germany. Side by side with decrees for the destruction of all signs of monarchy and feudalism, all gates, triumphal arches, coats-of-arms, and the statue of Louis XIV., and the bell that rang for St. Bartholomew's massacre, the *Moniteur* for Sunday, August 26, 1792, or more properly, "the fourth year of Liberty and the first of Equality," contains an account of an interesting and characteristic scene. Two days before, a deputation had waited on the National Assembly, urging that French citizenship should be bestowed on any author who had wielded his pen for the cause of liberty. The petition was vehemently supported by Chabot, the daring originator of the saying that citizen Jesus Christ was the first Sansculotte. A list was drawn up,* and Schiller's name was included, perhaps at the suggestion of Anacharsis Clootz, who, though he boasted himself "French in heart and Sansculotte in soul," was, after all, a German, and had certainly read the

---

* The list is of interest to English readers, and stands as follows, the mistakes in spelling being obvious :—"Priestley, Payne, Bentham, Wilberforce, Clarkson, Makintosh, David Villiams, Gorani, Anarcharsis Cloots, Campe, Corneille Paw, Pestalorri, Washington, Hamilton, Maddison, Klopstoc, Kocinsko, Gilleers (*i.e.* Schiller)."

Robbers, and perhaps *Don Carlos*. The diploma of citizenship, bearing the vague superscription, "Sieur Gille, publiciste Allemand," did not reach him till March 1798, too late for advantage or compliment. It was, indeed, a voice from the dead. Danton and Clavière, who signed the document; Roland, who wrote the accompanying letter; and Anacharsis himself, all had gone the same road to the scaffold. As Goethe said: "The only mercy is that the thing finds *you* still alive."

But for the present Schiller gained little more from these early revolutionary works than a very dubious reputation in the eyes of the rulers and cautious authorities who hold the purse-strings in the literary world. It is true that, in the autumn of 1784, he was introduced as a promising poet to Karl August of Weimar, who flattered the deep-rooted love of a title, and perhaps held out some promise for the future, by bestowing on him the meaningless rank of *Rath*, or Councillor. But his engagement as poet to the theatre at Mannheim had come to an end in August, and though in his sanguine way he at once conceived the idea of establishing a great literary periodical, to be called the *Rhineland Thalia*, yet the winter was passed and the spring far advanced before even the first number could appear. A week or two later, being again in very close straits, and entangled further in certain love affairs, especially in a dangerous friendship with Frau von Kalb, one of the most conspicuous of all those emancipated and enthusiastic ladies who play a rather pitiful part in the biographies of most of the German poets and men of letters of that time, Schiller availed himself of a scheme which had been gradually developing during the last few months. In the previous June he had received a letter from a small circle of friends in Leipzig, expressing the highest admiration for his genius, and enclosing a few touching little gifts such as were dear to German hearts. He had not answered till December, but since then the correspondence had become regular, and the friends, chief of whom was Christian Gottfried Körner, afterwards the father of Theodor, the famous poet-hero of the Liberation War, had engaged to advance money, and to share the risk of publishing the *Thalia*. Inspired by a refreshing confidence in friendship, a confidence in which he was never to be disillusioned, Schiller quitted Mannheim for Leipzig in April 1785, and in leaving Mannheim unconsciously left behind him the oppressive gloom and bitterness of revolt that had hitherto for the most part characterised his mind.

CHAPTER III.

IN the last movement of Beethoven's Choral Symphony, after a storm of struggle and chaos and passionate rejection, a voice is heard saying, "O friends, not sounds like these! but let us raise a strain more sweet and full of joy!" And then, quietly, and as though exhausted with the struggle, but now at peace, the new phrase is given out, and gradually the whole chorus joins in the triumphant song of Schiller's *Hymn to Joy* :—

> "Joy, thou radiant spark from heaven,
>   Daughter of the gods divine,
> We, with sacred madness driven,
>   Here approach thy glorious shrine.
> What the cold world's sword would sever*
>   Thy enchantment binds aright;
> All mankind are brothers ever
>   Where thou restest in thy flight.
> *Chorus.*—Men in millions above telling,
>   Join in rapture of embrace!
>   Far above yon starry space
>   Some dear Father has his dwelling.

* Slightly altered in the later version.

>   Who, in spite of Fortune's blindness,
>   Wins one other man for friend ;
>   Who has gained a woman's kindness,
>   Let him in our triumph blend ;
>   Aye—who can one soul whatever
>   Call his own in any land ;
>   And who never could, we sever
>   Him, poor wretch, from this our band.
> *Chorus.*—All that our great orb containeth,
>   Join to worship Sympathy ;
>   For she leadeth us on high,
>   Where our unknown Father reigneth."

This imitation of the two first stanzas of the hymn may serve to give the English reader some feeble idea of the spirit of the whole. It was written, probably near Leipzig, but perhaps at Dresden, within a few months of Schiller's departure from Mannheim; and the exultation that it breathes, the rapturous belief in the possibility and power of universal joy and love, the fervent insistence on the goodness of the Creator and the beauty of His works—all mark the measure of the change. The blind struggle was over; inspired enthusiasm succeeded to gloom; and the negative side of the Revolution, its savage destructiveness and despairing outcry against the hard limits of existence, gave place to the great constructive ideas and impassioned hopes that may well fill our more sober age with envy, no matter how deeply we have learnt to distrust them. Ignorance of history and of the laws of the human mind, its immense inertness and hardly perceptible growth, is always common; but in one age it produces only the spluttering anarchist, and in another it may give us Rousseau, Schiller, Shelley, and the other apostles of those bright visions that seem to throw a golden haze over that brief dawn of years when "to be alive was bliss, but to be young was very heaven."* This remarkable and sudden change in the tone of Schiller's works, though we may perhaps trace some forecast of it in a few of the earlier poems, such as *The Triumph of Love*, was no doubt greatly encouraged, if not actually caused, by the happier external conditions of his life between his arrival at Leipzig in April 1785, and his first residence at Weimar in July 1787. The greater part of the summer of 1785 was spent at Gohlis, a little village close to Leipzig, but in the autumn he followed his friends, Körner and his newly-married wife and her sister, to Dresden, where Körner had received a legal appointment under the Saxon Government. The little circle, numbering only five or six in all, lived on terms of the closest and most unembarrassed intimacy. They were bound together by a romantic friendship which may appear rather ridiculous to undemonstrative minds, but which was in reality singularly free from the absurdities that in those days commonly pervaded relationships of the kind. Körner, who was three years older than Schiller, must have been a rare mixture of shrewdness, high principle, and extraordinary unselfishness. Though himself inclined to letters, an eager student of history, and devoted to the facile speculations that then passed for philosophy, he was, above all, enthusiastically zealous for his friend's success. He not only supplied funds for Schiller's necessary expenses, and undertook the risk of the magazine—no light burdens for

* Wordsworth's *French Revolution as it appeared to Enthusiasts at its Commencement.*

the limited income of a petty German official; he not only urged Schiller at a later time to abide by poetry, whether it paid or not; he entirely effaced himself for his friend's greatness, and never showed a trace of envy. Acting as the outspoken and most judicious critic of Schiller's productions, he also became his adviser in the gravest crises of his life; and though his advice went the way of all good counsel, it may now be seen to have been wise in almost every case.

Under the warm influence of appreciation and daily companionship, Schiller's nature expanded as a plant in the sunshine. He was living within sight of the strange cliffs and wooded defiles of Saxon Switzerland; in the midst of a luxuriant and smiling country, thickly planted with cherry-trees and vineyards; on the banks of a noble and historic river, and in the close neighbourhood of a large but beautiful town that boasted itself the gayest and most artistic city of Germany. For nearly two years this happy life went on, interrupted only by fits of extreme depression—such as are not infrequent in all sanguine temperaments, especially during periods of occasional loneliness—and by one or two futile love-affairs, bitter for the time, but soon happily forgotten in the change and stir and expectancy of youth. His writing was not very copious, though plans for many future works were laid. The completion of the tragedy of *Don Carlos*, and some speculative essays in prose, were his main occupations; but two lyrics, belonging, probably, to the autumn of 1785, are too problematic to be left entirely unnoticed. One was originally called *Passion's Freethinking*, and was included, in much abbreviated form, among the *Poems of*

SCHILLER. 51

the Second Period, under the title of *The Struggle*, in the final edition of Schiller's works. The other was the well-known and beautiful lament, entitled *Resignation*, beginning with the often-quoted verse:—

> " I, too, was born in fair Arcadia's land,
> To me did nature too
> Swear at my cradle joys on every hand ;
> I, too, was born in fair Arcadia's land,
> But clouds of tears eclipsed the springtide's blue."

Both poems created some scandal at the time of their publication in the *Thalia*, owing to the embittered energy with which they appeared to reject the commonly received notion of virtue as implying self-sacrifice, abstinence, and renunciation of pleasure. It is true that *Resignation* will bear a very different, and perhaps nobler, interpretation, and that the warning of the "Genius" to the poet, in the closing stanzas, may, after all, be on the side of renunciation. "Two flowers bloom for man," he says ; "one is Hope, and the other Enjoyment. Let him who plucks one not desire the other. Let him who has not faith, enjoy. The doctrine is eternal as the universe. Let him who has faith, renounce. The world's history is the Judgment of the world." But if, as is usual, critics adopt the opposite meaning—namely, that pleasure should be seized whilst it passes, for self-sacrifice in the end remains unrewarded —it may be said that both poems are but the converse side of the Hymn to Joy, and express in a different form the same conviction of the delight and goodness of life, when life is not marred and blighted by uninspired duties and cold asceticism ordained by custom only. Goethe's incomparably grander song, *A General Confession*, may serve as an illustration of the same ethical point; and, without going too far into the regions of abstract morality, we may perhaps say that the apparent paradox is but a revival in modern form of the true doctrine of salvation by faith rather than by works. It is interesting also to observe how far removed Schiller was from the main principle of Kantian ethics, which in later years he satirised and misrepresented in the epigram:—

> "I love to serve my friends, and do it still
> With pleasure; so it seems I'm doing ill."
> "Yes, you must hate them, then your duty's clear;
> You do with loathing what was once so dear."

In the so-called *Philosophic Letters* that were mainly written at Dresden, and published in the *Thalia*, remembrances of long and earnest conversations between Schiller and his friend are embodied. These letters are supposed to be a correspondence between Julius and Raphael, two absent friends, on the most abstruse and intangible problems of human thought. Julius has been recently induced by his elder and more-advanced friend to lay aside his earlier views of the universe, and follow the guidance of reason alone. He is full of a tremulous joy at the shining prospects that open out before him. "I am on a level with kings!" he cries; "for is not Reason mine?" And at the same time it is significant that he rejoices exceedingly to have become "a citizen of the universe," instead of remaining merely a good son, a good friend, and a useful member of society, though the modern reader may be inclined to doubt where the advantage of the change exactly lay. He then bursts out into a rambling and erratic confession of faith, the general character of which may be conjectured from the following phrases:—"God and Nature are two exactly equal quantities;" "Nature is an infinitely divided God;" "If every man loved all mankind, each of us would possess the world;" or again, "I freely confess my belief in the reality of disinterested love. If that does not exist, I am lost. I give up the deity, immortality, and virtue. I have no proof for such hopes left if I cease to believe in love." Such vapid and unprofitable musings were supposed to do duty for true Philosophy, till Kant, with his growing influence, gradually rescued her name from inanity by sharply drawing the limits between speculation and knowledge. But for the time everything was hoped from Reason. She held the field; and it is difficult for us, who are now told that "she has thrown up the cards," that "she is in full retreat along the whole line," to imagine how indisputable her claims to omnipotence were then considered. Consequently, as is generally the case where belief in the ultimate power of reason is strong, we find in Schiller's writings hardly any trace of religion, in the ordinary meaning of the word. For such religious instinct as he had, he sought satisfaction in unworldly ideals of beauty, friendship, and elevated humanity. The powerful influence of such ideals on his mind, the belief in their sufficiency, and the expectation of their wide supremacy through the world, are illustrated by the conception of the Marquis of Posa, the principal character in the play of *Don Carlos*, that was written during the months of Schiller's residence near Dresden.

As has often been pointed out, and as was, indeed,

lamented by Schiller himself, one of the greatest faults of this tragedy is the want of unity due to the change that had come over the author's mind during its composition. The earlier part was, unfortunately, published during the period of dissatisfaction and revolt, whereas the later acts are full of the hopes and enthusiasms that came to reconcile Schiller to existence. Consequently the centre of dramatic interest is shifted, and Don Carlos, the supposed hero of the play, gradually gives place to the ideal and typical figure of Posa. Schiller was rightly never quite satisfied with the play, and it was altered two or three times; but, as far as the structure of the plot is concerned, it is doubtful whether the final alterations, especially of the last act, were really improvements. There is, at all events, much still that is confusing, unnatural, and deficient in motive throughout the whole tragedy. The action turns on the well-known myth of the love of Don Carlos for Elizabeth of Valois, who had been betrothed to him, and afterwards, for reasons of State, married to his father, Philip II. of Spain; and the object of the drama, in Schiller's own words, is to represent the conflict between a personal passion and a great enthusiasm, the enthusiasm being suggested by Posa, who successfully endeavours to obliterate the prince's fatal love for the queen by inspiring him with the ideal of a patriot king, and urging on him the duty of at once delivering the Netherlands from persecution. The tragedy consists in the failure of this noble purpose, which is thwarted by the intriguing jealousy of courtiers and ladies-in-waiting, and, it must be added, by the extremely Quixotic, not to say injudicious, behaviour of the two heroes themselves, whose motives for working out their own damnation in this headstrong manner are hardly sufficiently explained.

The whole construction is indeed awkward, and has an air of laboured manufacture. As in all the German classical dramas, the English reader is likely also to notice the want, in Carlyle's words, of "those thousand little touches and nameless turns which distinguish the genius essentially dramatic from the genius merely poetical. We have not those careless felicities, those varyings from high to low, that air of living freedom, which Shakspeare has accustomed us, like spoiled children, to look for in every perfect work of this species." Further, though in a historical drama we do not necessarily expect historic accuracy, it makes the humblest student's brain whirl to hear Don Carlos, who died in 1568, condoling with Medina Sidonia on the loss of the Armada, whilst Alva, at the same time, is not only alive but on the point of being sent to the Netherlands. But whatever may be the faults of the drama as a whole, and they are very many, the words put into the mouth of the Marquis of Posa will probably save it from complete oblivion, at all events for the student of eighteenth-century history. In Posa we seem to see the great Girondist leaders of the Revolution foreshadowed. He is as noble, as self-sacrificing, as full of amiable and sounding phrases, and as ineffectual. He introduces himself as "the ambassador of all humanity," for he has come to secure a merciful and righteous government for the Netherlands. His mind is open to all that is gentle and humane, and he responds to friendship's call with touching sensibility. Carlos and he lay aside all formalities with an oath of eternal brotherhood; they embrace frequently, fall on each other's neck in floods of tears, and, finally, by a rather complicated manœuvre, Posa sacrifices his life to save his friend—or so, at least, he fondly imagines. In his famous interview with Philip, he bears a sublime front before the tyrant; he is conscious only of the common bond of humanity and fellow-citizenship; he asks no favour, for already he enjoys the laws, and to him his virtue is indeed its own reward. He refuses to take service under the King, saying, in his magniloquent way, "I love humanity, and under a monarch I may love none other but myself." From his heart he pities a king who is raised above all human sympathy like a god. Nevertheless, violence is so far from him that he would not overthrow a monarchy, not even in pity for the monarch.

> "That rage absurd
> Of revolution that but weights the chain
> It cannot ever fully hope to break,
> Shall never stir my blood. This century
> Is not yet ripe for my ideal. I live
> A citizen of those that are to come."

But monarchy, though allowed to remain for the present —that is, till time should overtake the speaker's nobleness—was not to continue as a selfish and tyrannical institution. With the crude frankness of a candid friend, the Marquis reproaches Philip for his misgovernment of the Netherlands, and warns him that he will hand down his name to posterity as a counterpart of Nero and Busiris. In sharp contrast he proceeds to draw the golden picture of a Utopian king, who is but the highest servant of Liberty. The aim of such a king is to maintain the rights of each citizen; he will encourage freedom of thought and of action; under his rule the farmer, the painter, and the poet will pursue their occupations in uninterrupted peace, secure of just laws and government, leaving the direction of affairs of State to the monarch whose business it is to attend to them, whilst his reward is the applause of his own conscience, and he himself remains concealed from view and almost unknown, "the artist of the pleasantly deceived machine."

Under this lecture on the Duties of Government, so characteristic of the German political ideal, Philip maintains an air of humility and exemplary patience. Throughout most of the play he is indeed the gentlest of monsters; never did lion roar so like a sucking dove. We feel that if he were not Philip he would be Posa. But the difficulties of his unfortunate position have been too much for him; and, surrounded as he has been all his life by greedy courtiers, intriguing ministers, and compliant maids-of-honour, he has too often yielded to his worse nature, and has removed himself further and further from the common ground of broad humanity. As plots seem to thicken upon him, as his son's mad passion is revealed, and he is tempted to doubt even the fidelity of his queen, he recognises with horror the helpless loneliness of his position, and yearns to find one honest and pure-hearted man whom he may call a friend, someone who will speak to him the truth, uncoloured by ambition or selfish desire. In Posa he thinks that he has found an answer to his prayer. After the first interview he discards for him all his former favourites and advisers, and entrusts to his righteous direction the affairs of State and the intrigues of the Court. At last he seems to have secured the faithful service and honest companionship for which his inner soul had longed in secret; and the shock of the disappointment, when in hope of saving Carlos from further indiscretion, Posa clumsily resolves to draw suspicion on himself, hastens a catastrophe that falls as heavily on the king's proud and suffering heart as on any of those whose ruin seems to be more immediately involved. A few years after the publication of *Don Carlos*, when in France the noble ideals of a Posa were rapidly disappearing before the flood of violence, Schiller meditated writing a treatise in defence of Louis XVI., but the intention was, unfortunately, frustrated by that monarch's execution—a sad instance of the evils of delay. The idea was characteristic, and, if it had been carried out, we may suppose that he would have taken much the same grounds as in his description of Philip in *Don Carlos*. For to the German revolutionist even a king was a man and a brother.

From the general tone of the concluding acts of *Don Carlos*, and all the other minor works that belong to these years, we may perceive how great a change had come over Schiller's spirit from the days when he wrote the *Robbers*, and, as Heine says, was like a little Titan who had run away from school, taken to dram-drinking, and thrown stones at Jupiter's windows. He had now ceased to satirise the past or even the existent, and had turned, full of golden hopes, to the wide prospects of the future. The greatness of man and the love that should bind together the whole human race are now his themes. With impassioned exaggeration Teufelsdröckh once exclaimed that he would shelter all mankind in his bosom for its sufferings and its sins. Schiller also would have taken the human race to his heart, but it would have been for its joy and its greatness. Nothing short of humanity at large would satisfy him; he speaks of patriotism and nationality as old-fashioned prejudices, only fit for the childhood of nations. In the immediate future he can see the universal brotherhood of man attaining to fulness of joy under the gentle guidance of love, freedom, and rational speculation. In the opening stanza of the poem called *The Artists*, finished in 1789, he draws a picture of man as already standing in full beauty, with the palm of victory in his hand, on the verge of the century. He represents him as the heir of all the ages, with senses open to the world, endowed with intellect, full of gentle earnestness and peaceful activity, emancipated by reason, and sustained by laws, the lord and master of nature "who has learnt to love his chains." We, of a century later, read such passages, and hear of such brilliant hopes, with a melancholy smile. It is evident to us that the author of the bloodthirsty *Robbers* had but turned from one phase of unreality to another, and had now entered on the way that was to justify the shrewd saying of Madame de Staël, that Schiller lived, spoke, and acted as if wicked people did not exist. Ignorance of history, incapacity to follow the slow and patient method of scientific observation, and, what was worse, a kind of conjectural history evolved from amiable ideas and calling itself philosophic, were the sands on which these golden palaces of hope were built. Rhetorical phrases, such as

Rousseau's "Man was born free, and everywhere he is in chains," were treated as sober statements of scientific discovery. The thinkers and politicians of the movement were poets ; the poets were rhetoricians. With such watchwords as Natural Rights, Natural Religion, Love, Friendship, and the Brotherhood of Man, it seemed so easy to march in triumph straight to the millennium. Nor was the struggle altogether without result, disappointed as the exaggerated hopes have inevitably been. To enthusiasts like Schiller man will always owe a debt of gratitude for saving him from the indifference and inaction of the wise and prudent, and from the contempt of those who call him a worm.

In July 1787 Schiller broke off in the midst of a drama called the *Misanthrope*, that remains one of his few unfinished works, and taking with him the schemes of some proposed attempts at history and imaginative prose that might prove more profitable than tragedy, set out for Weimar. With Körner he maintained an almost uninterrupted correspondence, and they met occasionally, but he was destined never to return home to that friendly circle from which he had gained so much. The chief motive for his removal was a hope of patronage at the Court of Karl August, who had already shown him favour. He was rightly tired of living on his friends, and was anxious to escape from the network of debt that had now encompassed him for years. Weimar was the El Dorado of literary men with small requirements but smaller means. He hoped, also, to find stimulus in the contact with some of the most distinguished minds in Germany. But perhaps, after all, he was equally influenced by the desire of meeting there his dangerously fascinating patroness, Frau von Kalb, with whom he was encouraged to aspire to one of those strange triangular alliances too common in those days to provoke even a smile. The intimacy was re-established almost at once, and their relation was recognised and most considerately respected, as Schiller wrote to Körner, by a sentimental society fresh from the *Nouvelle Héloïse*. But before a definite arrangement for the future could be arrived at with the acquiescent husband, Schiller was happily saved from an impossible position by the counter-attraction of more wholesome affections.

At the time of his arrival in Weimar, Goethe was still away in Italy, and did not return till the following summer; but Herder and Wieland received Schiller graciously, and with the latter he soon became very intimate. His accounts to Körner of these and other celebrities of the place are written with a fine satirical observation only too rare in his works. *Don Carlos* was read at Court and at various æsthetic tea-tables, but without exciting much enthusiasm. During a brief visit to Jena Schiller made the acquaintance of Professor Reinhold, the ardent disciple of Kant, whose reputation he foretold would in a century have eclipsed the reputation of Christ —a singularly blind prophecy. The influence of such society, and of the whole tone of life in those two neighbouring little towns that prided themselves so highly on their culture, was at first inspiriting. The mere sight of men of high reputation and accomplishment encouraged him to persevere in the ways of greatness. But a restless dissatisfaction soon set in. Unworldly as he was, he felt himself too much a man of the world for that remote and unstirred atmosphere.

Politics hardly existed, and there were then no grand reminiscences in Weimar to fall back upon as a staple for conversation. Intercourse was therefore mainly limited to criticism and scandal; and in a society where intrigue was almost taken as a matter of course, and Gessner was considered a poet, both scandal and criticism must obviously have been too tolerant to be interesting. Schiller seemed too large and active for that petty world, and he did not altogether escape the blight of its self-consciousness and cultured mannerism. However, after a short excursion in the early winter to Meiningen, where his eldest sister was now living, and back again through the Thuringian Forest by Rudolstadt, where he met the Charlotte von Lengefeld who afterwards became his wife, he shut himself up almost entirely from Weimar society, and spent the long hours of the winter poring over folios and dusty authors in preparation for the historical works on which he had now embarked in earnest. In spite of Körner's prudent warning that he might be amongst the first in poetry, but in history could never hope to rise above the second rank, he was tempted to abandon verse altogether. He imagined that his mind was in danger of exhaustion, and that he turned to history for new ideas; but the other motive he assigned for the change was probably more genuine. It had been hinted that he was a mere dabbler in literary pursuits; poetry and imaginative work were described by some as "libertinage of mind;" and though specialism was not then so highly developed in Germany as it is at present, such a reproach is always keenly felt in a country where scholarship and learning are so general, and creative genius has been comparatively so rare. It was hard for Schiller, with his impressionable and sensitive temperament, to live at variance with his surroundings; and in the midst of pedants, the taunt of dilettanteism, whether justified or not, was sure to strike home. He was also approaching the age when the homage due to a scholar's devotion is more readily paid than in early manhood; and in attacking large periods of history with his usual fiery enthusiasm, he felt that at last he had reached something solid and above reproach. Having in mind his former investigations into the story of Don Carlos, he chose the Revolt of the Netherlands for his special study. He worked enormously, and in five or six months his history of the first few years of the revolt was practically ready for publication. It appeared in the autumn of 1788.

Meantime he had sought relaxation at intervals in continuing the imaginative story called *The Ghostseer*. The scene is laid in Italy, and the plot, which, like so many others of the time, was suggested by Cagliostro's adventures, turns on all manner of manufactured wonders and mysteries. There is a mysterious Armenian, an inexplicable beauty, a Prince, an English lord, an electric machine, strange murders, coincidences, troops of ghosts, and all the other properties belonging to the dismal and impossible tales that in the beginning of this century first attracted the attention of English readers to German literature. It almost seems as though Schiller was on the way to forestall Hoffmann, but he had not the true story-teller's or novelist's gift. His heart was not in the work; *The Ghostseer* remained without a satisfactory conclusion, and few modern readers would dispute Schiller's own judgment, that hardly any employment, not even writing love-letters, had entailed upon him such a sinful waste of time as scribbling at this fantastic tale.

When he called the writing of love-letters waste of time, Schiller was not speaking without experience. It has been mentioned that on his return from Meiningen in December 1787, he passed through Rudolstadt. He was accompanied by Wilhelm von Wolzogen, a son of his worthy patroness of earlier years, and was by him introduced to his relations, the Lengefeld family. The mother was the widow of an intelligent and upright forester of high connection and credit, and she was now living with her two daughters at Rudolstadt in peaceful retirement, enjoying the confidence of the little Court, and occasionally undertaking the management of the children there. Her elder daughter, Karoline, had already contracted a loveless marriage with Herr von Beulwitz, a well-meaning and sober-minded gentleman, who still continued to be her husband in name, though at last she procured a divorce and married her cousin, the Wolzogen mentioned above. He had long been among the open admirers of the large-hearted lady, who was far too emancipated to restrict her affections within the old-fashioned limits. On Schiller himself she cast her eyes as an interesting new receptacle for the sentimental philandering that she was pleased to call her philosophy; and he was so easily entangled in the customary jargon of free love, the sacred rights of passion, the mystic significance of friendship and the rest, that it sometimes seems as though it was the kindness of fate rather than his own good judgment that saved him from relationships as bewildering as those that existed in the Godwin family.

In a letter to Körner, after the meeting at Rudolstadt in December, Schiller described both the sisters as "attractive and pleasing without being beautiful." Yet the portrait of Charlotte, the younger of the two, has at all events some claims to beauty. A fine oval face, with bright but serious eyes and a smiling mouth, is overshadowed on either side by masses of dark and wavy hair, hanging in loose abundance over the shoulders. She is looking up with dreamy pleasure from a book that she holds in one hand. The dress is loosely laced in front, below a full white linen bodice, like a Swiss girl's. Both dress and book are significant. The family had been for some time in Switzerland, living close to the very scene of Julie's tender history. The sisters raved of Rousseau. After that romantic lake, how flat and stale appeared to them the uses of the little German town! Yet in Rudolstadt, if scenery made happiness, one might have thought it would be possible to be happy. Through a broad and fruitful valley, between pleasant meadows or high-wooded shores, the Saale comes sparkling down from the pine-clad uplands that form the water-shed between the tributaries of the Elbe and the Danube. Whirling round the corners as it winds, lingering under high banks in deep eddying pools, rippling over the white and yellow pebbles at the shallows, leaping down the long, low dams of ancient mills, spreading out in quiet inlets and back-waters thick with flags, sweeping under bridges of crumbling grey and yellow stone, or of deep brown wooden beams supporting a red-tiled roof to protect the village roads, in late

autumn surging onward in flood, and in early spring
strewing all its banks with blocks of blue ice three feet
thick, it presents every beautiful feature of a wild but
serviceable mountain river. It bears with it innumerable
rafts of pine from the hills where Jean Paul was born,
past many ancient and historic towns and cliffs crowned
with castles, past the fields of Lützen and Rossbach,
through the great northern plain to the Elbe and the sea.
The names of the little villages with timbered walls and
high-peaked roofs, clustering close round the church spires
so that none of the apportioned land may be wasted, tell
of the immemorial struggles of Hun and Slav and Teuton.
The long valleys and profound ravines that run up
amongst the mountains from the meeting-place of many
streams by which Rudolstadt stands, still breathed of old
German traditions and legends of witches and "the little
people." And scattered at wide intervals through the
forest-side, isolated and remote, stood the villages of the
rude Thuringian natives. Early bent and dried, men
and women alike, by poverty and the heavy labour of
the fields, renowned for their ugliness and stupidity,
speaking an incomprehensible dialect amongst themselves, and to strangers using a recognisable but peculiar
German, never having intercourse with any class but
their own, nor with any higher understanding than their
pastor's, who was but one of themselves, nevertheless
they were endowed with a childlike humour that almost
made them shrewd, a dogged, unreasoning patience, a
delight in the simplest enjoyments, in music, processions,
and open-air dancing on rough platforms decorated with
branches of fragrant pine, and endowed also with an
obstinate belief in the goodness of "the dear God," and

with an accumulated inheritance of neglect and wrong that might have saved them from the contempt of the cultured.

But the cultivated circle to which the sisters naturally belonged cared nothing for peasants, except in sentimental tales and sugared pastorals; and in spite of their enthusiasm for nature and its beauties, they suffered all the miseries of boredom. "It is true," Karoline wrote long afterwards, in what is perhaps still the best biography of Schiller, "it is true that there were in Rudolstadt plenty of men of science and culture; there was a gymnasium, a good library, a collection of engravings, a cabinet of natural objects—everything that could offer all the elements of a finished education; yes, and there were even a few poets besides," and yet they were not satisfied. They felt that somehow their society fell short of the standard of Weimar, Jena, and other neighbouring towns. Their persistent self-culture wanted the stimulus of kindred minds, and a field for display. They studied all the polite literatures: we find them reading Ossian, Fielding, Gibbon, Shaftesbury, Montesquieu, Tasso, and above all, of course, Plutarch and Rousseau. Karoline, as the philosopher, belonged to a Berlin "Band of Virtue," in which we must presume that the need rather than the possession of virtue was the qualification for membership. Its object was the propagation of mental and ethical culture. Lotte, the blue-eyed brunette of twenty-one, was mainly devoted to the arts of sketching and playing the piano, in which she seems to have attained rather more than the average proficiency of an amateur, according to the standard of the time, which indeed, in sketching at all events, was not very elevated, if we may judge from Goethe's highly-praised performances. But none of these pursuits, neither literature, nor philosophy, nor art, could altogether dissipate the cloud of dreariness that is nature's vengeance on the neglect of wholesome relations to her primal necessities. It is true that recently a romantic interest had arisen from Lotte's attachment to a British officer, who had been called off to the Indies, and left her to despair. But the melancholy of love only increased the evil by giving a recognised sanction to a life of tender emotions. Like so many others among the leisured classes of Europe, the sisters in Rudolstadt spent most of their time in contemplation of their own feelings. Sentiment was the only genuine interest, and from the exaggeration of its importance arose all those strange perversions of moral judgment that infected Germany perhaps more than other countries, so that even France was amused at its grotesque immorality. The weakness of the sentimental period, in spite of the common talk of virtue, friendship, and brotherhood, was in reality its intense egoism. "I thank heaven from my heart," writes Karoline on one occasion, after reading Mirabeau, "that no one dear to me has any connection with politics." Schiller describes himself as looking out upon politics and the life of action as from a nut-shell, where he is personally very comfortable. The ideal life of the true sentimentalist was to sit for ever at the coffee-table in the midst of a sympathetic circle, reading some touching author, or analysing his own heart amidst abundant tears. That Schiller ultimately saved himself from this enervating influence was one of his greatest achievements; and perhaps the highest honour due to the great names of Lessing and Frederick is that, insisting by example or precept on the primary necessity of action, they stood from the first like barriers of rock against the influx of this watery tide. It is comforting also to reflect that owing to the very exclusiveness and selfish pre-occupation of the sentimentalists, the heart of the nation was suffered to remain sound. It was only the small class with leisure for culture and boredom that really suffered.

On his first acquaintance with Rudolstadt Schiller had entertained a vague idea of spending the following summer there, to escape from the oppressive mental atmosphere of Weimar. The plan was naturally developed by the presence of Lotte herself in Weimar at the beginning of 1788. And, accordingly, in May we find Schiller at Volkstädt, a small village on the Saale, only a mile or so southward from the rock on which the great white Schloss of Rudolstadt stands overlooking the little town. Here he stayed through the summer, and in the early autumn removed to the town itself, so as to be still nearer to the household where he was so welcome. Nearly every evening was spent with the sisters, mainly in reading, speculative conversation, or some other form of intellectual pursuit. Homer and the Greek dramatists occupied them especially, though indeed Schiller's knowledge of Greek was even more limited than Goethe's, and, like him, he had to spell out the original text with the help of a Latin key. Nevertheless, he was justified in hoping that by these studies he might purify and elevate his own style, and with this view he ventured to translate some of Euripides, and then actually set to work upon the *Agamemnon*. In various literary schemes and productions the months passed happily away. Soothed by the beauty of the country, and by constant intercourse with sympathetic and admiring souls with whom he stood on the pleasant borderland between love and friendship, encouraged by the sense of his own growing powers, Schiller could enjoy a hopeful present unshadowed by remorse. He was near the end of his apprenticeship; he was still young; above all, he was still in good health. For mere happiness this was probably the best time in his life. In November he returned to Weimar, fully intending to renew the sweet experience in the following summer. But happiness does not repeat itself.

In poetry, the result of Schiller's work during all the time since his departure from Dresden was comparatively slight. He was, indeed, gradually approaching a period of almost complete silence in his art. Nevertheless, at Rudolstadt he wrote *The Celebrated Woman*, one of the best of his few entirely humorous works. It is a satire in verse, perhaps aimed at Sophie de la Roche, at that time probably the most notable woman of letters in Germany. It takes the form of a letter of condolence, written by the husband of an authoress to a friend whose wife has been guilty of ordinary infidelity. As consolation, the writer draws a picture of the far worse fate that had befallen himself since his wife, encouraged by the flattery of some renowned critic, took to writing books. She now belongs, not to him nor to another, but to the whole human race. With no further thought for her husband nor her children, she keeps her interest for the newspaper reviews, and her affection for the literary friends from whom she may hope for admiration. Deaf and blind to nature, except in so far as it may suggest a subject for some trifling poem, she wanders restlessly from place to place, vainly seeking to still the craving of her insatiable vanity, and depending for her poor chance of happiness on the passing whim of an ignorant acquaintance or a reviewer in a hurry. The whole is a fine satire on all, whether men or women, who regard the universe primarily as subject-matter for "copy."

There are also two serious poems belonging to this period, *The Gods of Greece* and *The Artists*, both very characteristic of Schiller's manner, and perhaps the most carefully finished of his earlier works. Both were contributed to Wieland's *German Mercury*—*The Gods of Greece* in March 1788, *The Artists* exactly a year later—and both really deal with the same subject, the all-importance of art and beauty, though the point of view is very different. The former is a lament for the vanished beauty of the old Greek mythology, or, rather, of the poet's idea of it. In contrast to the present aspect of the universe as a dull material system, directed only by blind, unswerving laws of gravitation and the like, or by a Ruler too remote and obscure for any human interest, a picture is drawn of the bright age of Greece, when the sun and stars, the trees and rivers, and all the world were alive with gods and heroes and fair spirits, and art and beauty still had power to turn inexorable fate, and "gods were more human and mankind more divine." In one form or another, the lament has been repeated by most of the greatest modern poets, from Wordsworth downwards; and generally, though not always, it has served to veil a blow at Christian pessimism, to which the melancholy and harshness of the present world is attributed.

In Schiller's case, considerable outcry was raised by the critics against the "heathenish" tendency of the poem, especially among the little clique of "Neo-Christians," in whom we may perhaps recognise the germ of the future Romantic School.

The Artists is not a lament but a song of triumph, as may be seen from the passages referred to earlier in this chapter. Yet the ultimate motive is the same as in the *Gods of Greece*. Man is great, but his greatness is due to art; and in the conjectural history by which this position is supported, Greece, as the home of art, naturally occupies the first and largest place. Beauty is said to be the sole guide to knowledge, and truth is only revealed to mankind under her mask. She leads man to duty along the paths of joy and freedom, and without the order and measure that she introduces into phenomena, nature would be a frightful chaos to his eyes. From art arose thought, feeling, laughter, and the purity of love. From art man built up his ideal of divinity, and by its aid he ventured to look beyond the grave. The principle of art has pervaded every detail of man's life, and to the hands of artists the dignity of man for the future is entrusted.

In these two poems some critics have perhaps rightly detected a personal side,—in the *Gods of Greece*, an elegy on the fair hopes and ideals of boyhood and youth, and in *The Artists* a confident determination to be true to art through good report or evil. Yet at the very time when Schiller was writing *The Artists*, he was preparing, though unwillingly, to abandon art for some years. During the winter 1788-89 negotiations were proceeding, mainly through Goethe's influence, for his appointment to a vacant professorship of history at Jena university. The professorship was "extraordinary," that is to say there was no fixed income, but the professor was allowed to make what he could from lecture-fees. Schiller hesitated for a time, knowing that the step would mean, as he said "a surrender of all joy for three years." His ignorance of the subject also gave him some scruple. But the necessity of securing some fixed position in life with a prospect of income, however uncertain, had now become very pressing. Hitherto, like Cæsar, if he wanted more, he had borrowed more; but most people come to a limit in that way of life. He calculated his expenses at Jena at 450 thalers (say £70) a-year, and, what with fees and money gained by writing, it seemed possible to win independence at last. Accordingly he accepted the proposal, though without enthusiasm, and set to work at once upon his first course of lectures, for which he chose the Introduction to Universal History as the subject. In May 1789. at the beginning of the summer "Semester," he settled in lodgings at Jena, and was duly installed.

CHAPTER IV.

THE ancient town of Jena, which was now to be Schiller's home for many years, lies on the Saale, only some twenty miles below Rudolstadt, so that Schiller might still hope to visit his friends there, even in the midst of professorial duties—for at first he lectured only two days a week. The bare hills by which the town is surrounded on all sides, except where the river has forced its way through, are of a loose and shaly formation, yielding easily to the wear of frost and water, by which indeed they seem to have been gradually converted into hills out of the great swelling table-land that rises slowly from Weimar, and is cut in half by the deep bed of the river. In consequence, the hills are flat at the top, and within about a hundred feet are all of the same height, so that they must have seemed monotonous and tame after the sharp crags and irregular mountains of solid rock in the wilder forest district round Rudolstadt. In the year after Schiller's death the north-west quarter of this undulating plain, beginning from the crest of the hill that overlooks Jena itself, was to be the scene of the annihilation of the Prussian and North German forces, a stern contradiction to all the high-flown prophecies of universal brotherhood and peace, a sharp, and, in the end, most salutary, lesson against the neglect of patriotism and public service for the comfortable and isolated life of sentimental feelings or philosophic dreams. But this rude awakening was still far ahead, and on Schiller's arrival, the old town, hemmed within the limits of its mouldering walls, still slept on, famous only for its plums and its University of dreamers. Under the enlightened government of Karl August of Weimar, the University was already conspicuous for freedom of thought and daring speculation, though the great names of Fichte, Schelling, Hegel, the Humboldts, the Schlegels, Novalis, and the Romantic School in general, Fries, Oken, and all its other professors or students who were destined so soon to begin the battle of philosophic systems, were still hidden in the future. Attracted by its fame, especially as the second home of the new Kantian philosophy, students already swarmed to Jena from all parts of Germany and from Denmark, Sweden, and the Baltic provinces. The "Sons of the Muses," as German students delight to call themselves in contrast to "Philistine" shopkeepers and men of business, numbered nearly a thousand in Jena at that time—that is to say, about a sixth of the whole population. They represented the most advanced phases of opinion, for the influence of Kant and his followers was beginning to produce a philosophic revolution that by its eccentricities of thought and conduct, and its destructive criticism of all laws and customs, whether social or religious, was in many ways a counterpart and continuation of the earlier movement of "Storm and Stress." Admiration, therefore, combined with curiosity, naturally led them to give a generous welcome to a new professor who was regarded as the chosen poet of freedom and revolt. To the students Schiller was still the poet of *The Robbers*.

At the first lecture the room he had chosen was incapable of holding all the students who came, and they had to pour out through the streets to the largest *auditorium* in Jena. And even there the crowd extended into the passages outside the door and thronged the window sills. Schiller was received with loud applause, and the introductory lecture, which he had carefully written out beforehand, was considered a great success. At night he was serenaded by the students, and at the second lecture nearly five hundred were present. As has been said, he had chosen Universal History as the subject of his first course, and in that he meant to include the main causes of the development of the European and some Asiatic races from barbarism to a civilised state. He seems, indeed, to have been aiming at the History of Civilisation (*Culturgeschichte*) as it is called in modern German science. Supposed extracts from his lectures, published in the *Thalia* about this time, treat of the influence of Moses, Solon, Lycurgus, etc., but not all of them are by Schiller's hand. He passed the ages in review, with increasing rapidity towards the end of the course, down to the time of Alexander. This was the first "Semester's" work, and it seems to have given much satisfaction. But in the second "Semester," which began in the autumn, the attendance was very poor, partly for want of due notice, partly because Schiller's lectures were not a part of the necessary University course, and the students could not afford to pay for mental luxuries. His audience dropped to thirty, and as his income as Extraordinary Professor depended entirely on fees, he was reduced to the straits of a Scotch professor whose subject is not compulsory for a degree. He calculated that the winter's work, with lectures every day of the week —five on general history, from the Frankish monarchy to Frederick II., and one on Rome—would only bring him in some £9 or £10, and for this he had sacrificed art and liberty. He bitterly regretted that he had ever come to Jena. If he could have maintained his freedom for another two years, he thought he would have been sure of some more lucrative and suitable appointment either at Mainz or elsewhere. It was difficult even in Jena to live up to his position as a professor and one of the most celebrated writers in Germany on £20 a-year, though it is true that £20 in Jena at that time would go almost as far as £50 in modern London.

Worse than all, he was betrothed, and there would soon be another to provide for besides himself. The betrothal had been at last arranged in the summer of this year (1789), a fortnight after the fall of the Bastille. "The news," writes Karoline, with the true sentimentalist's want of proportion, "seemed a foretaste of the victory of freedom over tyranny, and we rejoiced that it came at the beginning of a charming love affair." But the affair was in reality not quite so charming as it seemed to after-memory. For a time there was danger of rupture with Körner, Schiller's one true friend, owing to various suppositions of concealment and neglect that can easily be imagined. Frau von Kalb, who was just meditating an open divorce from her husband, and marriage with Schiller, naturally did not help to smooth the course of love. An alliance with a commoner was displeasing to all Lotte's relations, for she would thus fall from the caste of nobility, and lose the cherished privilege of the title *von*. Lotte herself also, who seems to have been endowed with a wholesome fund of simple sanity, was alarmed and distressed at Schiller's obvious attentions to her sister, their affectionate correspondence, their hopes of future happiness and life in common; nor can Schiller's attempts to reassure her be more fitly described than by the word *banal*. We must, of course, make some allowance for the absurdly exaggerated language of the time, else it would seem that he did not really care the turn of a penny which of the two he married, though he would have preferred to marry both. There were difficulties enough, therefore, in the courtship, but the most pressing, though, perhaps, not the most serious difficulty of want of money was partially solved by Frau von Stein, who, in her rambling old house, half mansion, half moated-farm, at Kochberg, only a few miles over the hills from Rudolstadt, had long been the intimate friend and patroness of the Lengefeld family. At a hint from her the Duke acceded to Schiller's petition for a fixed income at Jena, and granted him 200 thalers a-year (£30, or a little more). With Schiller's possible earnings by literature and lecturing, and an annual 150 thaler which Lotte's mother promised as dowry, it was evident that the little household might be established in a small way, without apprehension. Accordingly, in February 1790, the marriage was celebrated at the dilapidated little church of Wenigenjena, a poverty-stricken village across the river from the main town, where the fees would have been higher and the ceremony too public. In spite of the dangers that threatened it at the beginning, the marriage was unusually happy and successful, and its effect on Schiller extraordinarily beneficial.

The summer after the marriage was devoted to his second historical work, *The History of the Thirty Years' War;* and for the next two years historical subjects occupied him at intervals, though his interest in them steadily diminished under the attraction of studies to which his mind lent itself more naturally. Neither his capacity for history, nor his knowledge of it, had ever, in fact, been very high. When he accepted the professorship, he freely confessed that "many of the students would probably know more than the professor;" and at the same time he wrote in one of his letters: " History is only a storehouse for my imagination, and events must content themselves with whatever treatment they may receive at my hands." Such a method may be artistic or "philosophical," but it is not scientific, and, indeed, Schiller was only too much inclined to despise the patient investigators of historical science. In this, of course, he was not so blameable as the ignorant people who still continue to sneer at them as "horny-handed sons of toil;" for history, as we understand the word, was at that time only just coming into existence, and the invention of grand theories as to the meaning and purport of the universe and man was still considered more valuable than the most careful editing of a parish register. History was still entangled in the metaphysical stage, and was therefore largely conjectural. The difficulties of evidence and its relative value were not fully realised; writers were generally in too great a hurry, and too often contented themselves with second-hand authorities. The growth of such sciences as philology, comparative mythology, political economy, and of the whole evolutionary doctrine, has changed the ideal as well as the methods of history, so that we should not expect to find in Schiller the same object nor the same kind of work as in a great modern historian. But he fell short even of the standard of the times. His heart was not in the work, though he worked hard. It could not be said of him, as we read in one of his letters that it was said of Goethe in Weimar: "All that he was, he was with heart and soul." Indeed, the weakness of his position could not be better displayed than by the admirable passages in his Introductory Lecture, in which he contrasts the professor whose chief object is a competency, with the true scholar whose one and only thought is the advancement of learning. The former, he says, limits himself strictly to his little field, because from that alone he may hope for the substantial rewards of money or honour. When he has gained enough knowledge for his immediate purpose, he spends as little further trouble on it as possible; he becomes a violent opponent of all new departures and discoveries that may make his former labours vain; as he looks for reward only from outside, he is always complaining of ingratitude; and unless he reaps a harvest of gold, eulogy in the reviews, or favour from princes, he is overwhelmed by the misery of failure and disappointment. Schiller made it no secret that his first object in turning to history was to gain a competency, and unless he had been able to shake himself free from the whole subject, it may be feared that his account of the hireling professor might have served as a picture of his own fate.

As it happened, however, the study of history for these few years was, on the whole, advantageous, though the advantage was not unmixed. A mind always too apt to become rhetorical, diffuse, and vague, to lose itself in dreams and unrealities, gained from history substance, solidity, and a sense of outline. A failure to perceive or to represent the concrete was the weakness of German literature in general, and for this weakness history might be supposed to supply the next best antidote to life. Nor were the results of Schiller's labours in the subject destitute of intrinsic value at the time, though if he had produced nothing but his histories his name would probably have been forgotten long ago. We may well imagine that his lectures aroused, as we are told, the enthusiasm of the students by their freedom and breadth. His published histories also were received with general favour and applause for their interest and artistic arrangement, and for the beauty of the language, which is still regarded by many as the best model of German prose. Style and clearness were in fact the two points that Schiller was most anxious to secure. He wished to avoid the pedantry and the tediousness of ill-arranged and unproportioned detail that too often accompanied German thoroughness. In the introduction to the *Revolt of the Netherlands* he states that his object was to prove that history may be true without being a trial of patience, and may borrow something from poetry without becoming a romance. And in the *History of the Thirty Years' War* he endeavoured to ensure a still more popular and attractive tone, for, as he confessed to Körner, it was written expressly for dilettanti, being in fact contributed to a publication entitled *The Ladies' Historical Calendar.*

The subject of the Revolt of the Netherlands from Spain, which was intended to form one of a series of histories of the most remarkable rebellions and conspiracies, was suggested to him by his studies in Spanish history during the composition of *Don Carlos*. He based his work on Robert Watson's *History of the Reign of Philip II., King of Spain*, but most of the original authorities accessible in the library at Weimar and elsewhere were consulted, though some of the more valuable were unavoidably passed over owing to his ignorance of Dutch. The period was admirably suited to his special powers. The exuberant life and fantastic background of the Flemish towns, the startling incidents, the rapidity of movement, the personalities of tragic grandeur, characters distinct in themselves and sharply contrasted, all lent themselves readily to a dramatist's treatment. And then, too, the central motive of the whole, the struggle of an outraged people against the bigoted oppressor, for no mere national rights, but for the great ideals of Liberty in which the whole future human race had a stake, was exactly of the kind to appeal most strongly to Schiller's revolutionary enthusiasm. The history begins with a brief sketch of the Netherlands and their inhabitants from Roman times down to the accession of Charles V., and from that point the account of the events and the leading characters in the drama is continued, with increasing minuteness and interest, down to the departure of the Duchess of Parma and the arrival of Alva on his Catholic mission against the new religion. Here, unfortunately, the history comes to an end abruptly, so that in reality it forms little more than an introduction to the main story of the revolt. It was never finished, though fully elaborated accounts of the execution of Egmont and Horn, and of the siege of Antwerp, published some years later, prove that Schiller had not intended to leave it a fragment.

It was the same ideal of the struggle for Freedom that attracted him in the history of the Thirty Years' War, and his method of treatment is the same. The great figures of William the Silent, Philip, and Granvelle give place to Gustavus Adolphus, Tilly, Wallenstein, and Bernhard of Weimar. First we have a brief account of the effect of the Reformation on the political condition of Germany, and of the period between the abdication of Charles V. and the outbreak in Prague. The course of the war is then traced up to the landing of Gustavus, who is the hero or protagonist of the work. It is noticeable that the long period, from his death at Lützen to the beginning of the negotiations for the Peace of Westphalia with which the book concludes, occupies very little more than a quarter of the whole. And, indeed, Schiller's own interest in the history evidently flagged after the death of Wallenstein. Nevertheless, in spite of a too exclusive attention to what is merely interesting and dramatic, and in spite of a want of the strength and vividness that can only come from long intimacy with the original authorities, the book is still to be read as one of the best introductions to the study of the period. The clearness and brevity with which a confusing and tedious series of events is represented is both admirable and unexpected. The calmness and restraint of the style prove the author's increased self-control; at times, especially in the account of Wallenstein towards the end of his career, the language is almost Tacitean.

The two first books of the history, including the introductory period, and the account of the war itself down to the invasion of Gustavus and his victory at Breitenfeld, were published in September 1790, and the remainder appeared in the two following years. But in 1791 the course of Schiller's work, which he had estimated at fourteen hours a-day, was interrupted by the first attack of his fatal illness. He had gone to Erfurt for the New Year, and in coming home from the theatre one evening caught a feverish chill. After a few days of pain and misery the illness seemed to pass away, but only to return in the spring with extreme violence, so that for a time life was despaired of. It was accompanied by blood-spitting, horrible spasms in the chest and bowels, wandering of mind, and deathly prostration. Dr. Stark, at that time the most celebrated physician in Jena, and perhaps in Germany, attributed it to some disorder of the midriff rather than to disease of the lungs. A warm, dry climate was recommended, and, above all things, mental rest; but in Jena, where the snows in winter and the heavy rains in summer poured down from the hills upon the town as into a cup, and seemed to soak into the very bones of the inhabitants, it was hard to avoid rheumatism and chill, and for Schiller mental rest was impossible. Accordingly, it may be said that he never recovered, and this first attack was in reality his sentence of death. Even after the danger passed away for a time, some trace of disease was left that prevented him yawning or drawing a deep breath without acute pain; and when he was apparently fairly well, he would write that frightful spasms had kept him awake all night, and quite incapacitated him for work. For years he was never free from pain, and, worse than all, the disease brought with it the curse of tormenting sleeplessness. But what would have crushed the spirit of some men seems only to have strengthened and purified Schiller's. For besides the blessing of the sympathy of others with his suffering—a sympathy that, as Ferishtah said,* is the strongest bond of common humanity—he gained for his remaining years a high seriousness and devotion from the mere struggle with sickness and the knowledge that his time was short. It is possible also that the disease itself served to increase his eager activity, and fan his intellect into keener flame.

Beyond the continuation of his history, and some exercises in verse in the shape of translations, mainly from the second and fourth books of the *Æneid*; he was able to accomplish little during the remainder of this year 1791. In the summer he went to Carlsbad for his health, and took the opportunity to visit Eger, with a view to a future tragedy on Wallenstein, over which he was already brooding. On his return to Jena, the doctors still advised rest, but his resources had been brought so low that laborious production seemed to be the only alternative to destitution, when suddenly his cares were relieved by a most unexpected endowment of leisure. In the previous year, Jens Baggesen, a Danish poetaster, and a most ardent admirer of Schiller, had visited him in Jena, and had returned home full of his greatness. Having celebrated a solemn festival by the seaside on a false report of his death in the spring, he now, in December 1791, induced Frederick Christian, the enlightened and enthusiastic Prince of Schleswig

* Mr. Browning's *Ferishtah's Fancies: Mihrab Shah*, p. 56.

Holstein Augustenburg, to bestow upon Schiller the sum of 1000 thalers annually for three years, that he might have opportunity for recovery. The offer was accompanied by letters of such consideration and genuine esteem that Schiller could accept it without dishonour; and supported for three full years by what seemed to him the enormous endowment of some £180, which in Jena at that time would go about as far as £400 in modern England, he could now look forward with joy to freeing himself at last from all his old debts. and possessing leisure, as he proudly wrote to Körner, "to work for eternity." Perhaps the strangest part of a transaction, much of which seems strange in these days, was that he fulfilled his purpose.

Relieved from all immediate necessities, he now abandoned lecturing for a time, and hastened to finish off his history. In April 1792 he visited the Körners in Dresden, and in September his mother came up from Suabia to stay with the son whom she had not seen since his flight ten years before. She brought with her Nanette, her youngest daughter, who showed much talent for acting and the recitation of her brother's works, but died too young for anything more than promise. Whilst they were with him, Schiller was able to conclude his *History of the Thirty Years' War*, and so to lay aside history for ever. The announcement that in November he would begin a course of lectures on Æsthetics, showed the direction in which his real interest was now tending.

For some eighteen months past he had been studying Kant's philosophy in earnest. Both Körner and Reinhold had often urged it on him, and at last the attraction to the subject had become irresistible. The Kantian enthusiasm in Jena inevitably infected a mind always very sensitive to the influence of its surroundings. Even Goethe, who, in spite of his great diffuseness of interest, had far more self-restraint on the speculative side, was unable to remain entirely indifferent to a movement that made so much stir. For Schiller it was impossible to hold aloof. The modern German intellect is, as a rule, content to work its scanty plot of scholarship, science, or research, without troubling itself about the great truths that may lie beyond. Its study is of fact rather than of truth; and it has its reward in exactness, security, definite attainment, and other advantages. But Schiller, like many of his contemporaries, was impelled by a further desire, and longed to solve all difficulties and sound the most remote depths of existence. Unlike those of whom Schopenhauer says that they live not *for* but *on* philosophy, he was more than a professor; he was more even than a poet in the eager hope with which he rushed into Kantism. Its promises were so high. Setting aside both the facile scepticism and the speculative guess-work of recent essayists, it offered a new constructive system of genuine philosophy on the grand scale, extending its dominion over every department of human knowledge and action, stimulating to courage by insistence on the higher side of man's nature, checking presumption by demonstrating the strict limits of reason, and opening out vistas of hope in regions beyond the grasp of understanding. A peculiar poetic glow, arising from the sublimity of Kant's intellect and his moral strength of character, has been diffused over Kantism from the first; but to us it may seem strange that a system which, by its negative side, may almost be said to have laid the foundations of agnosticism, should at the beginning have resulted in the most extraordinary outburst of philosophic and poetic imagination. The youth and manhood of Germany were for the time genuinely inspired. After the crude theorising and ineptitude into which the dominant philosophy of Leibnitz, as interpreted by Wolff, had fallen, the very difficulties and obscurities with which Kantism was surrounded came like a rough but refreshing wind, bracing the mind to exercise. To Schiller, at all events, the strange terminology and super-subtle distinctions that seem so grievous a stumbling-block to other than German minds, proved no hindrance, but were attractive rather. Though not a philosopher, he had a natural inclination to things abstract, intangible, and remote; nor did he require the stimulus of the rewards that even an unphilosophic mind may gain from the study of Kant—delight in the sense of the power and solidity of a supreme intellect, in the passages of stern eloquence where the very strength of thought endues the rugged expression with grandeur, and in the fervour of living purpose which inspires and kindles the whole.

All the various parts of the system, however, did not attract him equally. The highest philosophic points in the *Critique of Pure Reason* were probably beyond his reach, for want of the necessary preparatory studies in metaphysics; and the high asceticism of the moral law, as laid down in the *Critique of Practical Reason*, seemed harsh and unnatural to a poet who maintained that "true human nature is always noble," and that virtue consists in following with pleasure a happy inclination to duty. As has been seen in the epigram quoted in the preceding chapter, Schiller considered that Kant exaggerated the rigour of duty, and he attributed this exaggeration to a natural reaction against the general laxity and hedonism of the times. His own sanguine temperament rebelled against the exclusion of pleasure from virtue; for, regarding mankind as an abstract ideal rather than a collection of frail and suffering individuals, he supposed the natural man to be endowed with a tendency to seek his happiness in good actions. "The good man," he says, "has a natural pleasure in good;" which is no doubt true, only the good man has first to be produced. But unless mankind was already embarked on the fair course of happiness and virtue combined, what was to become of all those high hopes of the speedy emancipation of the human race and the advent of the perfect millenium? Schiller, therefore, turned with impatience from what would now be called a "reactionary" theory of morality, such as Kant's, and hence we find him writing to Goethe: "It is strange and lamentable that this cheerful and jovial spirit (Kant) cannot wholly clear his wings from the dirt of life and certain gloomy impressions of youth. Like Luther, he reminds me of a monk who has thrown open his monastery, but cannot destroy all traces of it."

But though he gained comparatively little satisfaction from Kant's two main works, he plunged with undiminished enthusiasm into the one for which his mind was best prepared by previous training, the *Critique of the Power of Judgment*, in the first part of which Kant expounds his theory of Æsthetics, or the causes of the emotions raised by the beautiful and the sublime either in art or nature. The book had only appeared in 1790, but the comparative simplicity of the subject, and the wit and subtlety of the treatment, made it rapidly popular, and, in succession to the works of Baumgarten, Winckelmann, and Lessing, it became the text-book of subsequent German systems of Æsthetics, though time has proved that it was the second part, analysing the adaptations of nature as Teleological rather than Æsthetic, that contained in reality the more valuable results. Schiller soon became so engrossed in the subject that his correspondence with Körner was little more than a series of treatises on the nature of Beauty and its definition. At the same time, he was delivering his course of lectures on Æsthetics, and was beginning the series of prose essays on kindred subjects, published in his magazines, the *New Thalia* and the *Hours*, between the years 1792 and 1796. The scope of these essays may be gathered from the titles of the more important, such as "On the Cause of Pleasure in Tragic Objects" (1792); "On the Art of Tragedy" (1792); "On Grace and Dignity" (1793); "On the Sublime" (1793); "Letters on the Æsthetic Education of Mankind" (a series of twenty-seven, written to his Danish patron, published in 1795, but composed earlier); "On Naïve and Reflective Poetry" (1795-6). In the matter of nomenclature and, generally, of method, all these treatises were based directly on Kant; but how far they were consistent with his main conclusions, or might be regarded as fair corollaries to his system, was at the time a fertile subject of dispute. Many of the Kantians attacked them with great bitterness, and for the most diverse reasons. One of the critics, for instance, charged Schiller with only obscuring what, in a moment of paradoxical rapture, he called the master's heavenly simplicity. Fichte, on the other hand, whose contributions to the *Hours* Schiller had been obliged to refuse for their extreme difficulty, retorted that Schiller's essays were only fit for amateurs, being too clear, interesting, and artistic in form for the dignity of true philosophy. We may say, perhaps, that a careful selection from Schiller's writings would form a good introduction to Kantian Æsthetics for those who are unable to take the better way of approaching the fountain-head at once.

Most of the essays, however, have a value of their own apart from Kantian tendency, and some may still be read with profit. The treatise "On Naïve and Reflective Poetry," one of the last and longest, and by far the best of all, analyses and illustrates a distinction frequently insisted upon in the history of literature. By the Naïve is meant a quality that arouses in us a feeling of love and nearness to nature, as at the sight of children or young dogs. It consists in a contrast between art and nature, in which nature gets the better of art. It depends partly on a moral sentiment, partly on association and reminiscence, and, as it is the sign of an uncorrupted heart and of uncorrupted manners, it may sometimes seem strange and laughable, but never contemptible. It is too innocent for decency, and can never be morbid. It enters into the composition of all true genius ; and, like genius, it is not the result of principles, but the gift of heaven. We are always longing for it, but cannot attain it by seeking to return to the mere happiness of unintelligent existence. The naïve poet, therefore, generally appears at a comparatively early and uncorrupted stage of society, as in Homeric Greece or Elizabethan England, though in later times one may still be found here and there, hurrying across the world as a scared stranger among people who no longer comprehend his like. For the other class of poets who appear in a highly-civilised or sophisticated society, Schiller uses the word "sentimental," not in its usual bad sense, but merely as equivalent to "reflective." The sentimental poet, he says, *reflects** on his impressions, instead of stating them directly. In parting with nature man does not lose poetry, but becomes reflective, brooding over nature with a gentle melancholy, unknown to people like the early Greeks, who were themselves at one with nature, just as a sick man's longing for health is unknown to the healthy. The natural man is complete in himself, but the civilised or reflective man is always striving after an ideal he cannot reach; hence the ancients excelled in the finite, as in statues, whereas the moderns aim at the infinite, especially in poetry. This distinction, which Schiller proceeds to illustrate in various forms of poetry, such as satire, the elegy, and the idyll, is familiar enough to all critics and art students now. It corresponds loosely to the distinction, so often drawn since the time of the Schlegels, between the Classic and the Romantic, though the Romantic does not cover so wide a field as Schiller's conception

---

* This use may perhaps furnish the key to the saying of Goethe's that aroused some critical controversy a few years ago: "When he (Byron) *reflects*, he is a child."

of Reflective art.* Schiller also traces a somewhat similar antithesis in nature between beauty and sublimity, and in conduct between grace and dignity, especially in the æsthetic expression of the emotions, grace being freedom in voluntary action—a sign of a "beautiful soul"—dignity being mastery over involuntary action—a sign of a sublime spirit. But after all, these large divisions and classifications are often but puzzling guides, and perhaps the chief value of the essays lies in the occasional illustrations from contemporary literature, the admirable criticism on Goethe and a few other contemporary poets in "Naïve and Reflective Poetry," and the condemnation in the same essay of that German sentimentality from which Schiller had with difficulty escaped, and of the vulgarity that he represents as still supreme among the middle classes. In most of these writings also, though Schiller was always very careful to exclude all considerations of utility or morality from art, there is a distinctly ethical side, the connection being best represented in Schiller's own words to Goethe at a later time—words that recall the main position in the first part of Mr. Pater's *Marius, the Epicurean*—"Laxity in æsthetic matters always shows itself connected with moral laxity; and the pure, strict striving after what is highly beautiful will lead to rigour in morality also."

How far this excursus into philosophy and philosophic criticism was of advantage to Schiller as a poet, quite apart from the intrinsic worth of his æsthetic

* "The Classic I call the Healthy, the Romantic the Sickly," said Goethe. The distinction, like most other distinctions, had really been made by Aristotle; *cf. Poetics*, xvii., 2. εὐφυοῦς ἡ ποιητική ἐστιν ἢ μανικοῦ.

essays themselves, is too large a question to be fully discussed here. Philosophy has been till quite recently at once the glory and the plague of the German mind. In Schiller's time there was a growing tendency to become enamoured of obscurity, to discover difficulties where all had seemed simple, to divide what before was single, to kill the flower of pleasure by grubbing at its roots, to paralyse artistic production by dogmatising on the purpose and method of art. What artistic soul could listen without despair, or, what is worse, without loss, to this hideous terminology, to definitions that darken knowledge, to endless discussion on the subjective and objective, which in reality cannot be conceived apart, to solemn divisions between various kinds of reason and understanding, which in reality are all one? "Often," says Carlyle, speaking as a philosopher, "a proposition of inscrutable and dread aspect, when resolutely grappled with, and torn from its shady den, and its bristling entrenchments of uncouth terminology, and dragged forth into the light of day, to be seen by the natural eye, and tried by merely human understanding, proves to be a very harmless truth, familiar to us from of old, sometimes so familiar as to be a truism." Even for a philosopher, it seems too often to be a case of "so much for so little," and for a poet one may suppose the bargain would be harder still. Schiller himself, who had fallen only too easily into all the tricks of the metaphysical trade, had no doubt in later life of his mistake. In his correspondence with Goethe, his philosophic tendency was a subject of repeated lamentation. He well knew the weak points of his own mind. "I poetise when I ought to philosophise," he writes, "and I philosophise when I ought to poetise." Or again, whilst reading *Wilhelm Meister*, though he unfortunately persuaded Goethe seriously to diminish the value of the book by introducing various vague and philosophic absurdities, he was made painfully conscious of the unreality of the philosophic temperament compared to the purely artistic : "The poet is the only true man," he writes, "and the best philosopher is only a caricature in comparison." Nor did philosophic criticism fare better at Goethe's hands. "The demands made by criticism," the latter says in the same correspondence, "destroy the innocent productive state, and give us as genuine poetry something that is in fact no poetry at all. The *art* of poetry requires a certain good-natured narrowness enamoured of reality." Nevertheless we need not suppose that Schiller's study of Kant was all in vain. It saved him at all events from the vapid theorising of boudoir philosophy ; it encouraged his enthusiasm for noble ideals ; and together with his marriage, the increasing responsibility of his position, the approach to death, and the wisdom that came naturally with years of devotion to high pursuits, it contributed to the stability and seriousness of his subsequent life.

The lectures on Æsthetics that began in the autumn of 1792 suddenly collapsed in the following spring, owing to a violent return of illness that troubled Schiller at intervals all through the year, and made continuous work impossible. Professorial lecturing was, in fact, never resumed. A longing for the old Suabian land of his childhood came over him, and in August he started with his wife for Heilbronn. There was some doubt how the old Duke would receive the runaway army-surgeon of eleven years before, but though Schiller asked permission to enter the dominion with pardon for past offences, no notice was taken either of him or his requests, and he visited Ludwigsburg, Stuttgart, and even the "Solitude" without question. "The old Herod," as Schiller called him, with the ingratitude due to injudicious good intentions, was, in fact, occupied with very different interests from pursuing the vagaries of a random poet. The tide of war was flowing continually nearer to his boundaries. Already the wounded were coming in, and hospitals would have to be built. Besides, he was dying; and to die, as he told the parson, was no child's play. He was buried with due pomp in October, his virtuous Franciska alone weeping over his coffin. In the previous month Schiller's first child had been born at Ludwigsburg, and the family stayed in Suabia through the winter, for the most part at Stuttgart, within easy reach of Schiller's parents, who seemed to have entered upon a healthy and comparatively cheerful old age. There were other friends of youth to be visited, in most cases with some disappointment. In the course of years interests had diverged and run into different grooves; Schiller had himself become entirely devoted to intellectual pursuits, and in practice his sympathies were very narrowly limited.* He had some interviews, however, with Cotta, the bookseller, at Tübingen, and arranged with him for the publication of a new literary magazine, to be called *The Hours*, an arrangement that led to very important results for himself. In May 1794 the family returned to Jena.

* It was at this time that Dannecker modelled the bust by which Schiller's appearance is best known.

Schiller had now finished his apprenticeship, though he was not conscious of any change; he had made all his mistakes in life, and had wasted his powers for the last time. It had taken him thirty-five years to accomplish little more than finding out by toilsome endeavour where and how to begin. His health was hopelessly shattered; he was grievously discouraged, and hardly dared any longer to believe in himself. But the time of weakness and error was now to end, and, cheered by a friendship with a mind far greater than his own, but not too great to need his help, he was about to enter upon the eleven brief years that were left him with the self-control, security, and definiteness of aim that are the certificates of mastership in art.

CHAPTER V.

GOETHE'S intercourse with Schiller had hitherto been slight and distant. There was much both in mind and circumstance to keep them apart. After Goethe's visit to the Military Academy in Stuttgart, where Schiller was still an unknown student, the latter did not see him again till 1788, when a meeting was arranged at Rudolstadt by the Lengefelds; but the result was disappointing, as is generally the way with forced friendships. The fame of the author of *Werther* and the high report of him in Weimar—where, as Schiller writes, he was even more beloved as a man than as a poet—had perhaps raised expectation rather too high. At all events, in the account of the interview contained in a letter to Körner, of which the following is an abstract, there is little enthusiasm and already a trace of antipathy. "His first appearance," Schiller says, "was considerably disappointing; I had heard so much of this attractive and beautiful figure. He is of middle height, and stiff in bearing and gait; his face is reserved, but the eye very expressive, and one hangs with pleasure on his glance. In manner he is very earnest, but good-tempered and kindly. He is dark, and looks older than he is. His voice is remarkably pleasant, and his narration flowing, spirited, and full of life. One listens to him with extraordinary pleasure, and when he is in the mood, he likes to talk, and talks with interest. . . . He speaks of Italy with passionate remembrance. . . . On the whole, my really high idea of him has not been diminished by personal acquaintance; but I doubt whether we shall ever approach very near each other. He has already outlived much that is still interesting to me, much that I still wish and hope for. He is so far in front on the road that we can never meet; and his whole nature is differently constituted to start with; his world is not mine—our modes of thought are essentially opposed. However, after one such interview one can't be sure; and time will show."

In a later passage from the letters to Körner (March 1789) we find impotent jealousy added to natural antipathy: "This man, this Goethe, is once for all in my way, and he too often reminds me how hardly fate has dealt with me. Destiny has borne *his* genius lightly forward, whilst I have had nothing but fighting and striving up to this very minute." But this was perhaps written in momentary vexation or despondency, and in the following extract (November 1789) we may see in brief the real grounds of opposition that in after times gave not only critics, but the poets themselves, so attractive a subject for mental analysis. After a conversation with Goethe on Kant, Schiller writes: "It is interesting to see how Goethe clothes everything he has read in his own manner and style, and gives it back as a surprise; but I shouldn't care to contend with him on subjects that touch me very nearly. He has none of the enthusiasm that openly professes attachment to a cause. To him all philosophy (or truth) is subjective, and that of course ends all conviction and disputation at once. Nor can I quite approve of his philosophic method. It too much derives from the world of sense what I derive from the soul. But his spirit works and investigates in every direction, striving to construct a whole for itself; and that, in my opinion, makes him a great man."

Goethe, on the other hand, deliberately held aloof. To a man who attached so much importance to right judgment in art, Schiller's reputation could only be repellent. In a well-known passage in his *Annals* he has described his despair at finding, on his return from Italy, that whilst he himself was full of new ideas of art, new standards of perfection, and a profounder reverence for the classical, the whole German world, including his most intimate friends, had gone mad on *The Robbers*. In Schiller he only saw the embodiment of that spirit of moral paradox, sentimentality, unruly passion, and formless production from which he had at last succeeded in purifying himself. The popularity of such a work made him despond of German taste, and, joined with the powerful attraction of natural science, almost persuaded him to abandon art and poetry altogether. Nor had Schiller's subsequent writings, such as *Don Carlos*, or the philosophic essays, altered this unfavourable impression. The admixture of Kantism and abstract philosophising had only made agreement appear more impossible. Besides, during the earlier years of Schiller's residence at Jena, Goethe was much away from Weimar, either in Saxony, Silesia, or with the armies on the Rhine; and year by year he was devoting himself more exclusively to physical experiments in botany, anatomy, and the science of light and colour. It certainly seemed as though he might safely be content to avoid a University professor whose views and manner of life were equally opposed to his own; who was ten years his junior; who had tried his hand at drama, rhyming, history, and philosophy in turn, had been successful in all, but had touched perfection, as Goethe understood perfection, in none. Yet out of elements so unpromising the most renowned fellowship in literature was to arise.

It came about through the *Hours*, the magazine that Schiller had arranged in Suabia to edit for Cotta. On his return he sent out notices soliciting contributions from all the names most distinguished in Germany in science or letters; amongst the others was one addressed to Goethe in formal and respectful terms (June 13, 1794). After consulting with friends of Schiller as to the prospects of the adventure, Goethe replied with a promise not only to contribute, but also to give advice as to the management of the undertaking. It was just at this time also that an accidental meeting at a scientific society led to the famous conversation that may be regarded as the beginning of their friendly intercourse. The following is an abstract of Goethe's account of the matter in his *Annals:* "I found Schiller once at a meeting of the Natural Science Society, and it so happened that we came out together, and began talking of what we had heard. He seemed to have been interested, but remarked with much insight that this disjointed way of dealing with Nature was far from encouraging to a layman. I answered that perhaps it was not altogether pleasant even to the initiated, and that there might be another way of representing Nature, not as split up into departments, but working in full life and energy from the whole into the parts. He wished for further explanation, but could not see how such a method could proceed from experience. I was tempted into his house, and there explained to him the metamorphosis of plants, and delineated a symbolic plant point by point before his eyes. He followed it all with great interest and decisive intelligence, but at the end he shook his head and said: 'That is not experience, that is an Idea!' I was a good deal annoyed, for in these words the line that separated us was clearly shown; however, I collected myself, and answered: 'Well, it's a great comfort to have Ideas without knowing it, and actually to see them with one's eyes.' The disputation was continued with vigour on both sides, and ended in an armistice, each of us thinking himself invincible. But the ice was broken. Schiller had great powers of attraction, and held all who approached him under a spell. His wife, whom I had known and esteemed from her childhood, contributed her share to a lasting friendship. And so, owing to that great controversy between Subject and Object, a controversy that perhaps will never finally be settled, we concluded an alliance that remained unbroken, and conferred much benefit on ourselves and others. For me especially it was a new spring in which everything burgeoned into glad and abundant life as from opening seeds and budding branches."

In the matter immediately in dispute, Schiller was probably right as far as the correct use of terms went, but he failed to recognise the great significance of

Goethe's conception as a step in the theory of development. Mere differences of philosophic method, however, could no longer separate men who, by increasing intercourse, became more and more aware of the real identity of their aims and meaning. The famous correspondence that was to extend to a thousand letters, or perhaps more, and was to form a treasure-house of criticism for Germany almost equal to the *Conversations with Eckermann*, began at once, and developed rapidly after a fortnight's visit that Schiller made in September to Goethe's house in Weimar. From that time the friendship was secure, and it only ended at Schiller's death. Each, as he wrote to Körner, could give the other something that was wanting, and receive something in return. The good fortune that is part of greatness had in fact brought them together just at the crisis when for the first time intimacy was possible. Schiller was in the common but pitiful position of an author who cannot think of his past works without a spasm of disgust and loathing. Sick at heart, insecure, dimly conscious of a change, but still uncertain of the path he was to tread, he found in Goethe solid support, encouragement, and an unfailing guide. Confirmed by the friendship and applause of a man of the highest genius in an age fruitful in intellect, he could no longer entirely distrust his own powers, though he could now, in a letter to Körner, admit, without a pang of jealousy, that compared to Goethe he was but a "blockhead." His whole existence took a new and stronger tone, and from this time onwards he could at length rank as a great writer. Even on his bodily health his wife and others always noticed the beneficent influence of

Goethe's presence, so sane and wholesome and outwardly serene. And yet it is certain that the advantage to Goethe was at least equally great. He too was discouraged, and was exposed to the dissatisfaction that haunts a creative mind when it ceases to create. He was falling a prey to his natural temptation—to diffuseness and mere observation. Indifferent to fame, raised above reach of poverty's incentive, humbled by continual contemplation of nature's vastness, he had gradually ceased to appeal to the outer public, and his inner circle of friends was becoming exhausted, or, for one cause and another, was falling away. They no longer supplied the stimulus he always required for production. He, too, had been passing through a time of change, but his old acquaintances could not recognise its meaning, and since his return from Italy he had been living like one who, having visited the upper sunshine, had gone back to dwell in the shadowy gloom of the Platonic cave. "Then," he says, "came my relation to Schiller, the greatest blessing fortune has given me in my later years." Or again: "He saved me from the charnel-house of science, and gave me back to poetry and life." He continually speaks of this friendship as a "new life," a "second youth." "You have given me a second youth," he writes when he was forty-nine, "and converted me again into a poet which I had as good as ceased to be." New hopes arose, and he was braced to fresh endeavours. Passive indifferentism gave way before the eager enthusiasm and concentrated energy of this younger friend and rival. Schiller's entire freedom in discussing future literary plans contrasted with his own invariable silence, and other similar differences of thought and manner were in themselves refreshing and stimulating. It required continued exertion to keep up with Schiller's restless progress. "Every week," Goethe said to Eckermann long afterwards, "every week Schiller was a new and more complete man. Each time I saw him he appeared to me to have advanced in reading, knowledge, and judgment. He was a magnificent creature, and was taken from us at the very height of his powers."

As to the comparative merits of the two, whether as poets, thinkers, or men of letters, few whose opinion is worth listening to would now think of raising the question, but would rather content themselves with the saying of Goethe in old age: "For the last twenty years the public has been contending which was the greater, Schiller or I, and they ought to rejoice that they have two such fellows to contend about." The present age, at all events, if it attempted to deal with the question at all, could only wonder that any answer but one was ever for a moment thought possible.

Meantime Schiller was engaged in the tormenting work of bringing out the first number of *The Hours*. The prospectus promised well, and subscribers came forward rapidly. As it was proposed to exclude all matters of pure scholarship, religion, and politics, the contents were practically limited to literature and a few branches of science and philosophy. Besides Goethe, most of the greatest names in Germany were actually included in the list of contributors, or could probably be depended upon. There was Wilhelm Humboldt, Schiller's closest friend and warmest admirer in Jena; and there was his brother Alexander, afterwards the great traveller and man of universal knowledge, who promised papers on geology; there was the new professor, Fichte, whose connection with the magazine was soon to be rather roughly severed, as mentioned in the last chapter; and Garve, the veteran philosopher; and Gleim, the veteran poet; and Herder, already touched with the bitterness of disappointed and reactionary middle age; and Jacobi, for ever searching shadow-land for the lost convictions of his youth; and the young brothers Schlegel, sons of stage-thunder. The remuneration was high, higher, it was said, than German publisher had ever offered before, and to the editor himself Cotta was most generous. The enterprise was started under excellent auspices, and yet from the beginning it brought nothing but disappointment. Schiller was exposed to all the misery and irritation of any one who has to trust to others for his success. Irresponsible, careless, crazy with self-importance, the so-called contributors seem to have been as troublesome a herd as ever a distracted editor had to drive. Some pleaded sickness, some were too idle to write at all, some hesitated till it was too late, some preferred to watch a while how the adventure succeeded; others, possessed partly by conceit, partly by the common idea that the editor would himself enjoy the perusal of their dissertations, overstept all limits of space. Schiller slashed away bravely; Goethe said of him that he was especially good at cutting down, and that he once saw him reduce a contributor's poem of twenty-one stanzas to seven without the smallest loss. But he does not mention whether the poet in question was of the same opinion, nor estimate the effect of such proceedings on Schiller's popularity in literary circles. And to the woes of an editor he unwisely added the weakness of a contributor, thus exposing himself to all the hostile criticism and unworthy imputations of the dissatisfied and rejected. Worse than all, the public grumbled at the result, and not without reason. Of the great names put down in the prospectus, only a few actually wrote, and they did not suit the popular taste. Goethe's first contribution was voted dull at the beginning and enigmatic at the end—and, indeed, it was both; Schiller's *Letters on the Æsthetic Education of Man* were unintelligible to the many, and insufficient to the few. The bad name that the first issue won for itself clung to all subsequent numbers. It was in vain that Schiller turned to poetry again, and contributed the earlier of the poems now published as of the *Third Period*. It was in vain that Goethe sent his *Roman Elegies;* they, in fact, only aggravated the wrath of the growing and influential band of mystics and neo-Christians, who afterwards publicly burnt *Wilhelm Meister*, up to the sixth book, and now were loudest in the cry of heathen immorality. Equally in vain, Schiller, in hopes of relieving the heaviness so much complained of, began the publication of a story by his sister-in-law, Caroline, who had at last secured a divorce, had married her lover Wolzogen, and was living for the most part in Weimar, gradually discovering that even a love-match does not ensure joy for evermore. The public grew more and more ill-humoured, and with every number subscriptions fell off, till at last, after three years' existence, the magazine, at Schiller's own request, was quietly allowed to collapse. It must be owned that he was not a model editor. Besides such obvious indiscretions as forcibly breaking off stories, or a series of articles, in the middle, he made the economic mistake, common to many whose interest in a publication is ideal rather than material, of supposing that the general reader will buy what is thought to be good for him, rather than what he finds genuinely attractive.

But long before the enterprise was given up, the two friends had taken full vengeance on their critics. In a passage in his *Annals* Goethe has described the confused and perplexing condition of German thought at this time. All was anarchy and chaos. There was no recognised standard either of taste or truth, but all the thinking and artistic world was divided into jealous little groups that watched each other with the scorn and bitterness natural to intellectual cliques. Three such groups had rendered themselves specially hateful to Goethe and Schiller through their general absurdity, combined with continued attacks upon the *Hours*, and disparagement of all that the two had recently produced; we may call them the Mystics, the Philistines, and the Metaphysicians. The Mystics, who devoted themselves to an indistinct neo-Christianity and theosophy that was in the end merged in the Romantic movement and the Catholic reaction, were mainly represented by the Counts Stolberg, two brothers with whom Goethe had been intimate years before; but Lavater, half apostle, half charlatan, would probably still have been acknowledged by the whole mystical body as their high priest. From Berlin, again, old Nicolai still proclaimed himself the champion of the hosts of ancient Philistia and common-sense, and appealed to the memory of his fallen comrades against the perplexing innovations of genius and time. And, thirdly, on every side, possessed by philosophic frenzy, the flock of metaphysicians was floating upwards into the inane, darkening the air with shadowy wings, and distracting the reasonable mind with hoarse and unintelligible cries.

Towards the end of 1795 Goethe, (or perhaps Schiller, for the point is disputed,) conceived the idea of inflicting some penalty on all such people by means of a series of satiric verses to be called *Xenia*, or "parting gifts," a title borrowed from the thirteenth book of Martial's epigrams. He hoped thus to deal a blow at the absurdities and exaggerations of the various contending schools, and at the same time to expose the superficiality that he detected in all departments of learning, especially amongst reviewers, journalists, and editors, who were by their very position compelled to pretend to more knowledge than they possessed. He also dreamed of rousing the German public from the stupendous dulness before which, for many years, he had stood aghast. "Germans," he wrote to Schiller a little later, "are everywhere accompanied by platitudes, as the English by their tea-pots." The epigrams were to act as Samson's fiery foxes amongst the standing corn of the Philistines. Schiller eagerly embraced the proposal. Like most idealists, he had an inborn faculty for satire, and Goethe used to say that Schiller's epigrams were far sharper and more biting than his own. It is, indeed, by no means difficult in many cases to distinguish the authorship of the various *Xenia* by difference of style, and German editors at a loss for a subject for their research have spent a great deal of time in separating them according to evidence or conjecture, in spite of Goethe's own condemnation of the attempt as the depth of Philistinism. He points out how unimportant success would be, even where possible; for the epigrams were genuinely the joint work of both poets, and, in fact, sometimes one would suggest the idea, and the other would put it into verse. They were all written in the same metre, the elegiac distich, a metre not quite so harsh and impossible in German as it would be in English, and they were all published without sign of authorship, though other collections of epigrams that came out in the same periodical were distinguished by the initials *S.* and *G.* They appeared in the Autumn of 1796, in the *Muses' Almanack* for 1797, the second number of an annual of verse that Schiller had undertaken to edit in spite of his difficulties with the *Hours*. It survived some four or five years, and holds a high place in the history of German poetry.

The authors had originally intended to publish a full thousand of *Xenia*, and to effect some sort of unity by arrangement; but they wearied of the joke when little more than four hundred had been written, and these appeared very loosely grouped together. For us it is hard to realise or to comprehend the extraordinary excitement that their publication produced in the German literary world. We in England have been spoilt by richer fare, nor do we readily appreciate the kind of satire to which the German mind seems to be most sensitive. Besides, the hard fate that inevitably attends all such productions as the *Dunciad, English Bards and Scotch Reviewers,* or Mr. Lowell's *Fable for Critics,* has befallen the *Xenia* also. Though some few familiar names may be recognised in the satire, the greater number of its victims are only known to the minute student of forgotten literature, and to him are of interest only because they were victims.* The thought that the satire may keep their memory alive for an extra century or so, does not, however, soothe the wounded breasts of the failures in literature; and after the publication of the *Xenia*, Goethe and his new comrade, who had both already experienced something of the envy, hatred, and malice that characterise the inferior literary temperament, were exposed to the combined fury of all the assured mediocrities, the superficial journalists, the cranky enthusiasts, and the hole-and-corner *Ratés* in the German states. *Anti-Xenia* appeared on every side, and Goethe and Schiller were personally attacked with all the rancour of jealousy and wounded self-conceit. Unfortunately, Goethe's unconventional domestic relations gave the enemy an opportunity that was eagerly seized; but the grossness, dulness, and absurdity of the answers are in reality the highest evidence of the superiority of the *Xenia* themselves.

The following rough imitations of some of the epigrams upon fairly familiar names may perhaps serve to give the English reader some idea of the method employed. Here, for instance, are two out of the thirty or forty directed against Nicolai, who, it must be remembered, was always appealing to his friendship with Lessing in old days as a confirmation of his own greatness :—

* " Pretty ! in amber to observe the forms
Of hairs, or straws, or dirt, or grubs, or worms !
The things, we know, are neither rich nor rare,
But wonder how the devil they got there ? "
Epistle to Dr. Arbuthnot.

> "Speak not of Lessing; here he suffer'd scorn;
> But in his martyr's crown thou wast the thorn;"

and:

> "So blind you are, unless you touch, you cannot understand;
> And what you touch is foul'd and smudg'd by contact with your hand."

Or again, on Lavater:

> "'Man's a poor creature!' Yes, I know; and wanted to forget it,
> And came for comfort unto you, and deeply I regret it;"

and:

> "Great indeed is the gulf from grandeur down to inanity:
> To bridge it over in man, Nature inserted—vanity."

On Count Stolberg, who had exclaimed against the heathenism of Schiller's and Goethe's poems:

> "For insults to the gods Apollo hurled you down
> Parnassus: so you've won in Paradise a crown."

On the Schlegels:

> "What only yesterday they learnt, they teach to-day without a question.
> O what a blessing it must be to have so rapid a digestion."

The epigram on Wieland, always so dainty, flighty, and capricious, comes under the constellation Virgin in the series on the Zodiac:

> "Bow down yourselves, as well beseems, to Weimar's virgin lady:
> And if she pouts—for beauty's whims a pardon's always ready."

On the commentators of Kant:

> "'Tis strange how one man's wealth the need of many assuages;
> And when a monarch builds, the hodmen get good wages."

On Wolf, who had recently published his famous *Prolegomena* to prove that the *Iliad* and *Odyssey* were collections of the works of several different poets:

> "Seven towns once strove for Homer as their own;
> A Wolf now rends him, and gives each a bone."

Some of the *Xenia*, on the other hand, as well as all the series of epigrams called *Votive Tablets*, written by Schiller, and published at the same time, were more general in tone. The following may be taken as examples:—

On the present generation:

> "Of such a time as this I never have been told,
> When age alone is young, and all the youths are old."

On his belief:

> "'Which religion do you profess?'
> 'Well, really, I cannot tell;
> None of all these, at least.'—'Why not?'
> 'I love Religion too well.'"

On the Genius with torch reversed, a Greek symbol of death, rendered very popular by Lessing and Herder:

> "The boy with torch reversed
> Is lovely and poetic;
> But, my masters, death
> Is scarcely so æsthetic."

On Expectation and Fulfilment, a verse that reminds us of the last page in Mr. Browning's *A Soul's Tragedy:*

> "Out to the ocean steers the youth
> With many a gallant mast;
> Silent, with one poor boat scarce saved,
> Puts in old age at last."

To a Philanthropic Reformer (1795):

> "'To serve mankind,' you say, 'I gave up all;
> Vain was the effort, my reward was hate.'
> I'll tell you how with men it doth befall;
> And trust my saying, it's as sure as fate.
> Think of mankind as highly as you may,
> Wear him within your heart, your deeds will prove it;
> And to the man who meets you on life's way,
> Reach out a helping hand, and he will love it.
> But rain and dew and your reforming passions
> Best leave to heaven's own ways and good old fashions."

To a Dilettante:

> "Because your verse runs smooth in some long-cultured tongue
> That rhymes and thinks for you, have you the gift of song?"

On the common fate:

> "We hate each other, we strive, we're always ready to fight,
> And all the time your hair, like mine, is turning white."

To the Ilm, Weimar's little river, from a series on the rivers of Germany:

> "Small is my stream, but as it glides along,
> Its wavelets hear full many a deathless song."

On Science (or Knowledge):

> "To one she bears a goddess' name too high for tongue to utter;
> And to another she's the cow that gives such first-rate butter."

It may be doubted whether satire has any good effect upon the immediate objects of its scorn. It is only too likely to harden self-assurance into perversity, and for reasonableness to substitute personal hatred. Who were these two, cried the second-rate authors in sympathetic chorus, that they should set themselves up as the final court of literary judgment? The "Jachin and Boaz of the Temple," Herder sneeringly called them, in anger that his place at Goethe's side had been taken by a younger and brighter rival! Nevertheless, though the production of inferior literature was probably but little checked, and hostile criticism against the authors of the *Xenia* was enormously increased, something had been gained. The partnership of the two friends had been proclaimed to the world; and they were now bound together by the two strongest ties, common action and common danger in the face of the enemy. And, what was more, they were themselves stimulated to further production; they were forced to silence cavil, as Goethe said, by their own Protean activity under good and noble forms, and so to rebuke all detractors. For both it was a time of extraordinary fulness of energy, and for Schiller especially the years from 1795 to 1798 were by far the most fertile period of his life in all forms of his poetry except the dramatic. During this time he produced nearly all his most celebrated lyrics and ballads, and it is of interest to watch the rapid growth of his art under the influence of Goethe's clear and comparatively realistic understanding. In the poems of 1795, contributed to the *Hours* of that year, or the *Muses' Almanack* for 1796, we still find traces of the old philosophic habit, allegory, symbolism, mythological personification, vague abstractions of various kinds. Yet the growth of power, of directness and self-restraint, is obvious in such poems as *Ideals*, in which the poet again laments over the golden hopes of youth; the *Dignity of Women*, a popular source of German quotation; *The Veiled Image at Sais*, an allegory on the danger of irreverent search for truth;

The Dance, unfortunately written in elegiacs; and *The Walk*, also in elegiacs, but a very characteristic work, in which the poet rather loosely describes the scenery of the Saale valley, and the thoughts of man's history and development that are called up by it;—similar speculation, as we have seen, was not new to him, and was not improbably suggested by Herder's *Ideas on the Philosophy of the History of Mankind*. In the same year he also wrote *Pegasus in Harness*, in which he describes the winged horse put up for sale at a market, harnessed to a post-cart, then to a plough, with great disaster in both cases, till he is rescued by Apollo himself, and soars with his rider into the clouds. Körner objected that Pegasus ought to have died of hunger; and, indeed, the parable would then have been more exact. One of the most popular of this series, and thoroughly in Schiller's manner, is called *The Partition of the Earth*, and represents Zeus as distributing the various sources of wealth among the different classes of men, such as the farmer, squire, priest, merchant, and king. At the end, the poet arrives from a far-off land, and finds nothing left. In reply to his lamentations, Zeus asks him where he has been all the time. "I was in thy house," answers the poet:

> " Mine eye hung on the blessing of thy sight,
>   Mine ear on thy celestial harmonies,
> O, pardon thou the soul that with thy light
>   Was blinded, and forgot all earthly ties ! "

> "What can I do?" cried Zeus, "the world is given;
>   Its fruit and wealth no longer I command.
> But wilt thou dwell with me in this my heaven,
>   Whene'er thou com'st, the doors shall open stand."

But in the meantime, whilst the poet was claiming a title to abodes beyond the clouds, misery was beginning to settle down upon his old earthly Suabian home. At the very time when his productive power seems to have been at its height, during the very months of 1796 when he and Goethe were preparing for the onslaught upon stupidity in general, blow upon blow was falling upon the unhappy family near Stuttgart. For two or three years past the state had been uneasy with impending danger from without and within. After the old Duke's death things went from bad to worse. The tide of French ideas was forcing its way even into the stagnant places of the Suabian peasant's heart. He did not get so far as beheading his masters, but he shot their hares, and who could say where that would end? The shoemakers were growing restive, and in that part of Germany the ruling classes had uncomfortable associations with the Shoe.* Troops were called out, but they were soon needed for other foes than their own countrymen. The French were threatening to swarm across the upper Rhine by every passage, and Germany was beginning to pay for her long mistake of nominal federation and separate rule, for the ancient greed of her aristocracy, and the inert indifference of her middle classes. With natural injustice, the heaviest penalty was exacted from the innocent. The Duke retired to a neighbouring state to watch events; people of culture, like the Wolzogens, flitted to other centres of light; whilst Major Schiller, who had devoted his whole life to exact and regular accomplishment of every detail in his public

* From the time of the revolutionary League of the Shoe, and the early Peasant Wars,

duty, remained at the "Solitude," crippled with rheumatism and internal disease, and exposed to all the horrors of a French occupation. In the Spring his two unmarried daughters were stricken with hospital-fever, and Nanette, the youngest and brightest of his children, died. A few sentences from a letter to Schiller from his mother may give some idea of the misery of the time :—

"My dear son, our woes are inexpressible; we are all going to ruin. Your father's pains still go on. For twelve weeks we have had fires and lights burning day and night. He pours out groans and lamentations so that we don't know what to do for distress; he can't keep anything on. O God, we are all going to ruin; I can't bear it much longer. Distress and care, and the loss of dearest Nane that makes my heart bleed, prevent me hoping for any more content. Your father has quite forgotten her already. Ah, our dispositions are endlessly varied, and, my dear son, he has brought all his own and our misery and sorrows on himself. We often implored him with tears to take better care of himself; but it was no good. Last summer whilst he was rearranging the Tree-Nursery, he used to stay there from four in the morning till late at night in spite of mist and rain, and now he won't rest, and is wild with impatience because he can't get out. He is quite worn away. But when his pains stop, he's cheerful enough."

Schiller, too ill and weakly to go to their assistance himself, sent all the money he could, and induced his married sister, Christophine, to leave her melancholy old librarian at Meiningen for a time and help her mother with the nursing. She was there when Moreau's troops actually arrived (July 1796), after the defeats at Kehl and Ettlingen had left the whole of Suabia exposed to the French, and for a whole day she and her sister hid in a hollow under a bridge in the woods for fear of the savage and ill-disciplined soldiery. The day before, the house had been plundered of everything that was left in it down to the sick man's last shirt. Excitement and indignation completed the work of disease; he lingered a few weeks longer, and in the beginning of September he died. The mother went to live at Leonberg, and in 1802 was buried in the churchyard at Kleversulzbach, where her remaining daughter Louise had married the village clergyman.

During all this time, and, indeed, throughout life, Schiller's power of abstracting himself from the paralysing influence of external sorrows and cares was very remarkable, and on the whole to be envied. Though profoundly distressed at the unhappy condition of his parents and sisters, and harassed at home by the usual anxieties of a growing family, he was for the most part able to continue his labours both as editor and poet with at least as much energy and enthusiasm as before. As, however, his own health was continually failing, he removed, in the Spring of the following year (1797), from the house in the narrow streets of Jena to another about two hundred yards outside the town-walls to the south. It stood in a garden of its own, at the bottom of which the Leutra, a little tributary of the Saale from the hills on its left bank, has cut itself a deep channel through the rock. Above the brook a summer-house had been built, commanding a view, uninterrupted then by any embankment or railway station, over gently rising fields and orchards to the pine-covered heights of the Forst; and on the other side, to the hills beyond the river. Here he worked, or conversed with a friend. "In this bower," said Goethe, as he sat in it with Eckermann thirty years afterwards, "on these benches now almost broken down, we have often sat together by this old stone table, and exchanged many a good and great word. He was then in the thirties, and I in the forties; both still full of high aspirations, and that was something. All that is past and gone; I am no longer what I have been, but the old earth still holds together, and air and water and ground are still the same."

Schiller had hardly settled in his new home, when with his usual energy he set to work upon poems for the next year's *Almanack*. He and Goethe determined to try the effect of a series of ballads, partly as a contrast to the *Xenia* of the preceding volume. The ballad was not an entirely new form to Schiller, but he had attempted it very seldom, and it might have been supposed that his introspective and meditative cast of thought rendered him entirely incapable of the simplicity and directness that are the essence of ballad poetry. But though in nearly all his ballads there is some trace of this failing, that prevents them rising to the supreme perfection of Goethe's *King of Thule*, *Bard*, or *Erlking*, we cannot but wonder at the versatility and copious resource displayed in this sudden self-emancipation from reflection and philosophising. Between June and September 1797, he had produced the best and most familiar of those ballads that have become part of the necessary education of the German youth, whilst some of them are almost as well known in England. They are all based on some legend of classical or mediæval history, and the narrative is told, in most cases, with great fulness of detail and plentiful description. The metre employed is not the simple four-lined form used in the finest early German ballads, such as Tannhaüser, and in modern times with such

effect by Coleridge and Heine, but in most cases a long
stanza of six, eight, or even twelve lines, such as was
common in Germany from the end of the fifteenth
to the beginning of the seventeenth centuries, especially
in religious and political poems. In substance, perhaps,
their defect as a whole, if defect must be sought, would
be found to lie in a certain coldness. They do not
quite succeed in reaching the deepest springs of emotion.
Into what a different region we seem to come as we
pass from Schiller's *Knight Toggenburg*, or *Hero and
Leander* to the pathetic *Lament of the Border Widow:*—

> "But think na ye my heart was sair,
> When I laid the moul' on his yellow hair?
> O think na ye my heart was wae,
> When I turned about, awa' to gae."

or to the simplicity and terror of the words :—

> "Why did you melt your waxen man,
>   Sister Helen?"

As two representative ballads out of the six or seven
written during the summer of 1797, *The Diver* and *The
Cranes of Ibycus* might be selected. *The Diver* was the
earliest of them, and for power over words and grandeur
of description—as in the famous lines on the whirling
gulf, or the youth's account of the monsters and vague
horror of the sea as he clung to a rocky ledge fathoms
down overhanging the immeasurable depth below—it is
unsurpassed by any that followed. The legend on which
it is founded occurs with slight variation in Italy, Sicily,
and Spain, but the immediate source from which
Schiller drew is unknown. The myth of Ibycus and
his avenging cranes is also Sicilian, and is mentioned

by Plutarch, but was probably derived by Schiller from Fazelli, a Sicilian historian of the last century. In the ballad we see Ibycus the poet on his way from Rhegium to Corinth to take part in a contest of song. As he approaches the city, he greets, with hopes of good omen, a flight of cranes that have followed him from the south. Suddenly in the solitude of a wood he is set upon by two murderers and slain. As he dies he calls upon the cranes to avenge his murder. His body is found, and all the Greeks, assembled for the festival, lament his loss. The theatre is crowded for the religious drama; they come from Athens, and Aulis, and Phocis, and Sparta, and from the opposite coasts of Asia, and from the islands. The chorus of avenging goddesses enters with solemn tread. They are wrapt in black; torches are in their hands; snakes hiss in their hair. They chant the strain of slow-footed retribution that dogs the flight of the guilty and never rests.* As they slowly vanish in the background, the people sitting hushed, there is a whirl of wings and a sudden cry—

"See there, see there, Timotheus,
There are the cranes of Ibycus!"

The murderers have betrayed themselves; they are hunted out, and the charge of the cranes is fulfilled.

The other ballads of these months were *The Glove*, in which an irregular metre is used with great skill in adapting sound to sense, but the effect is spoilt by the harshness of the ending, as taken literally from the original French story, with its suggestions of the vulgar

* Schiller derived their chant from his friend Humboldt's translation of a chorus of the *Eumenides*.

cry, "Serve her right;"—a cry so beautifully reproved by Mr. Browning in his noble poem on the same theme —telling of the lady who for once took her knight at his word, and asked him to risk his life for her sake, by bringing her glove from the pit of lions, and so discovered the worth of knightly vows; *The Ring of Polycrates*, a version of the well-known story of Herodotus; *Knight Toggenburg*, a legend of mediæval constancy, the immediate origin of which has not been traced, though there is a similar story of Rolandseck on the Rhine; and *The Way to the Forge*, a French story of innocence protected and the guilty punished as though by heavenly intervention. In the same series there is one that is not a ballad, but may perhaps be imitated here as a proof how far Schiller could now depart from his earlier manner both in style and choice of subject. Goethe told Eckermann he considered it one of Schiller's best poems, and he only wished he had made a dozen like it. It is a semi-humorous Indian Dirge, and the idea was derived from John Carver's *Travels through the Interior of North America.*

"There he sits upon his mat,
  See, he sits upright,
With the very mien he had
  Whilst he saw the light.

But, O where the strong arm's sway?
  Where the mighty stroke,
And the breath that yesterday
  Blew the sacred smoke?

Where the eyes, like hawk's to view,
  That upon the face
Of the prairie wet with dew
  Spied the reindeer's trace?

These the legs that ever sped
  Swiftly through the snow,
As a stag with branching head
  Or a mountain roe.

This the arm that stiff and strong
  Strung the stalwart bow;
Ah, its life was not for long,
  See, it hangeth low.

Joy to him! he treads the ways
  Where no snow can fall,
And the fields are full of maize
  Growing free and tall.

Where the birds fill every bush,
  And the game the wood,
And the ponds are full of fish
  In a merry brood.

With the gods above he feeds,
  Leaves us mourning here,
Bids us praise his warlike deeds,
  And adorn his bier.

Gather gifts from far and wide,
  Raise the last lament,
Let us bury at his side
  What may give content.

Lay the axe beneath his head
  That he wielded strong,
And the flesh of bear, and bread,
  For the way is long.

Lay the dagger, whetted keen,
  That, from foeman's crown,
Quick, with just three strokes between,
  Severed hair and bone.

Colours too to dye his skin
Place beside his hand;
Red as flame he'll enter in
To the spirits' land."

Schiller's ballad literature was continued in the following year (1798) with *The Fight with the Dragon*, the longest and, perhaps partly for that reason, not the most successful of the ballads. It is founded on a story of chivalrous heroism and the discipline that punishes even noble but irregular achievement, and was taken from the records of the Knights of St. John. *The Surety* or *Damon and Pythias*, a legend of Sicily in the time of Dionysius (probably the Younger), to be found in the *Fabulæ* of Hyginus, was composed immediately afterwards. It is the story of a youth who, having failed in an attempt to murder the tyrant, is condemned to death, but allowed three days' grace to attend his sister's wedding, provided he leaves his friend to suffer in his place if he does not return. The interest of the tale lies in the constancy with which the youth overcomes the unexpected hindrances that arise in his way, and is enabled to reach the town again just in time to deliver his friend from the executioner, and by this proof of loyalty and honour to appease the monarch's natural wrath.

In later years Schiller returned occasionally to the ballad form, as in *Hero and Leander* (1801) and *The Count of Hapsburgh* (1803), a legend of Rudolf, the first Hapsburg Emperor, derived from Tschudi's *Chronicon Helveticum*, which Schiller was then studying for his drama on William Tell; but after 1797 his real interest was centred in the drama, and he was able to pay but small attention to the lesser kinds of poetry, which in fact he had always theoretically despised in comparison. And yet to these later years his most beautiful lyrics also belong; and even here, though of course not so plainly as in the ballads, the beneficent working of Goethe's influence may be traced. They have not, it is true, the intensity, the depth of simple passion that give Goethe the highest place as a lyrical poet; nor have they his reach of thought, his profound human sympathy, nor his natural music. But next to his and Heine's, they are still the best German lyrics, and such love-songs as *Expectation* (or *The Tryst*) (1796), *The Girl's Lament* (1798), and *The Lover by the Stream* (1803), such poems as the *Mountain Song* (1804), a description of the St. Gotthard, showing Schiller's skill in realising the reports of others, *The Girl from a far-off Land* (1796), the *Dithyramb* (1796), and the lovely lyric called *Longing* (*Sehnsucht*, 1801), will bear to be named with the highest.

Of that section of Schiller's works which is generally published as "Poems of the Third Period," the remainder is chiefly made up of a few survivals from the album-verses in which that generation delighted, a few so-called "occasional" poems, and a considerable number of short poems in German elegiacs, of which the *Nenia*, a lament over the fugitive nature of beauty, is as beautiful an example as any. There are also some rhymed proverbs and sayings of wisdom, and a series of fifteen *Riddles* (1801-4), mostly descriptive of natural objects or seasons, some of them very gracefully written. The following is an imitation of the fourth:—

"There stands a bridge of pearly hue
  Above the waters grey;
A moment builds it up anew
  To dizzy heights of day.

The highest masts of vessels high
  Pass under it with ease;
No burden on its arch may lie;
  As you approach, it flees.

It rises with the stream, and fades
  Soon as the waters dry.
Now tell me, where's this bridge of shades,
  And whom it's builded by?"

But such poetic trifles were only allowed to occupy brief moments of Schiller's leisure from what was now to become the almost exclusive interest of his life. He was to end with drama, as he had begun. For some years he had been haunted by the idea of a drama on the life of Wallenstein, and in 1796 had begun working at it fitfully without any satisfactory result. He was hampered by the conception of another tragedy to be called *The Knights of Malta*, which was finally abandoned, though large fragments remain. In *Wallenstein* he was a long time making up his mind as to the best dramatic motive. He puzzled himself by a study of the *Poetics*, and by tormenting questions as to the proper sphere of Fate in tragedy. As Goethe said to Eckermann of his friend, "he had no repose in his nature, and could never be done with a thing;" his production was never quite inevitable and unalterable. Under Goethe's encouragement and advice, however, being reminded that "until a work of art actually exists, no one has any conception of its possibility," he settled down to the task in earnest in 1798. In October the Weimar theatre, which had just been restored on a grand scale, was opened with *Wallenstein's Camp*. *The Piccolomini* followed in January 1799, and *Wallenstein's Death* in April.

CHAPTER VI.

THE tragedy of *Wallenstein*, as is well known, is divided into three sections, generally represented on successive nights, and called *Wallenstein's Camp*, *The Piccolomini*, and *Wallenstein's Death*. It is not, however, on that account, a Trilogy in the Greek sense of the word, though it is often said to be. It is only a divided play. No separate part has any completeness in itself, and the division is entirely due to the portentous length of the drama, which not even a German audience could be expected to sit through without a break.* The separation of *The Piccolomini* from the main tragedy was indeed a device adopted, almost at the last moment, at Goethe's suggestion, in hopes of clearing the ground; for Schiller was deplorably encumbered and confused by the mass and breadth of his material. The division is consequently rather arbitrary, and might be made almost equally well at the end of a later act, where in fact it was made in the earlier editions. In a true Trilogy, where each of three plays is independent and complete, with a beginning, middle, and end of its own,

* Schiller calculated that the *Piccolomini* alone would take four hours. "If it begins at 5.30, people can get home by ten," he writes.

such an alteration would obviously be impossible; and, as far as form goes, *Wallenstein* can only be regarded as one great drama, in which the author has been unable to keep within the strict limits of theatrical representation drawn by the physical endurance of the actors and the audience. By the introduction of episodes, by the fulness of detail, and the length of the speeches, the treatment of the central subject, indeed, becomes epic rather than dramatic, and thus inevitably loses in power on the stage. But *Wallenstein* is nevertheless the grandest national drama that Germany has yet produced; and, as Coleridge has said, we must judge it with the feelings of Germans, to whom the great names and events with which it deals have long been familiar.

The tragedy of the hero's fall and death is admirably introduced by the gay and stirring scene in Wallenstein's Camp at Pilsen on the borders of Bohemia. It is written after the manner of the Meistersingers, in loose octosyllabic rhymes, suited for rough comedy or satire, and Schiller never surpassed it in vigour, life, and wit. It reminds us of the scene in *Faust* on Easter-day outside the city walls. The object of the whole is to represent the condition of Germany about the middle of the Thirty Years' War, and to give grandeur to the main action by showing us that the fate not of one hero only, but of an army, if not a nation, is involved in the issue. Kings do not fall alone, and we see in the *Camp* that to his army Wallenstein is a king. The rude soldiery confide in his greatness and believe in his fortune. Loyalty to his name is the one bond of cohesion and unity in all the chaos of a vast mercenary force, consisting, not of fellow-countrymen fighting side by side with stern resolution for their homes and the existence of their race, but of paid soldiers of fortune, drifted together from all quarters of Europe, careless of their cause, devoted only to the general by whose genius the army had been created, and on whose fortune must depend their chance of a gay and adventurous life, with plenty of excitement and plunder. Nor is this loyalty entirely selfish; the camp abounds, it is true, with all the characteristic vices of a standing army in which the soldiers do not serve from a sense of national duty or from national compulsion, but merely because war is their profession; it abounds in greed, frank debauchery of all kinds, and disregard of life. But beneath all this there lies the one wholesome principle that after all makes them an army, not a rabble—an unreasoning, uncalculating worship of Wallenstein himself, for whose honour we feel that at any moment the most selfish of them would go cheerfully to death. In their eyes he is almost equal to the Emperor in rank, though supposed to be his servant, and he is far above the Emperor in power and reputation. They will hear no word against him. They delight to recall his deeds and the greatness of the army in earlier and happier days when, as he himself says in a later passage—

> "Our life was but a restless, onward march,
> And like the roaring of the homeless winds
> We stormed across the war-affrighted world."

Those days were now passed and gone; the army was not what it had been when the Emperor's confidence was still unshaken and their leader's name as yet unassailed by malignant jealousy. Uneasy apprehension of change now troubles the air. There are rumours that, under various pretexts, the Imperial Court intends to divide and break up the army by degrees. The hearts of the veterans are heavy and disturbed; like trusty dogs, they vaguely feel the coming evil, and restlessly gather more closely round their master, looking up to him plaintively for encouragement and guidance, but only waiting for the moment when they may turn savagely in his protection upon the open foe. Wallenstein has forged the army like a weapon to his hand, and long trial has only proved its temper. If he is false to the Emperor, it might seem that the army would only think it true allegiance to follow him in treason. If he falls, he will not fall alone.

This is the serious note that runs through the merriment of the *Camp*, and prepares us for the tragedy. It is like the sense of thunder in the air on a full summer day, but it is not suffered to cloud the present gaiety of the scene. The curtain rises upon the noisy confusion of a *Marketenderin's* tent; soldiers of every race and uniform are drinking, gaming, and swearing; and originally one of Goethe's inimitable soldier's songs was sung at the beginning. A simple old peasant, who has been ruined by the prolonged wars, tries to avenge himself with loaded dice on the men who have caused his misery. Soldiers exchange their plunder, and cheat each other if possible. There is some rude flirtation with the *Marketenderin* and her niece. Some headlong chasseurs and a strict old quarter-master, who is the one serious character in the camp, dispute on the merits of new and old fashions in warfare. Interspersed with all the wild talk and confusion, reminiscences of past scenes of destruction, prowess, and excess, are introduced, giving the audience an idea of the previous course of the war and the temper of the time; and ever and anon the name of Wallenstein emerges like a distant and mysterious star, and we hear of his power, his assurance of victory, the enchanted ointment that protects him from wounds, his knowledge of the reading of the future by the heavens, and his dealings with the world of spirits. All swear that through good and evil report they will abide by him, and own no other command. A half-drunken recruit rolls in from some neighbouring town; he has left his shop to join the army; his family follow him with pitiful protests in vain. A sharp dispute arises over the right of courting the girl of the camp; in the midst of a dance she runs away; a chasseur pursues, and by mistake catches a fat old friar, who rushes in when confusion is at its height and pours out his celebrated sermon in the wildest doggerel:—

> "Hullo, hullo! Here's a pretty go!
> Here's a fine to-do! But I'm here too!
> This is no Christian army, I doubt;
> Are we Anabaptists or a Turkish rout?
> What! are you making the Sabbath a joke,
> As though God had the gout, and would fail of his stroke?
> Is this the time to be swigging and drinking,
> And sitting at table and wine-glasses clinking?
> *Quid hic statis otiosi?*
> Why stand you here with hands in your pockets,
> Though the Danube is plagued by the war-fury's touch,
> And Bavaria's bulwark is loose in the sockets,
> And Ratisbon's caught in the enemy's clutch?

> While the army lies here in Bohemia's valley,
> And troubles its head but to fill its own belly,
> Cares less for beacons than beakers of beer,
> Wets its lips, but a sword will not whet, never fear."

In a series of monstrous puns and coarse illustrations he then draws a picture of the miseries that the war has brought upon the Empire, the manner of his absurd eloquence being an exact reproduction, rather than a parody, of the sermons of old Father Abraham à Santa Clara, in whom the spirit of Jean Paul appeared a century before its time, with humour immature, and girded about with a Jesuit's frock. Twelve volumes of his extraordinary outpourings, including a circumstantial and edifying biography of Judas Iscariot, have come down to us, and it was from one of them, sent him by Goethe only a week or two before the *Camp* was acted, that Schiller conceived the idea of introducing the Friar's sermon, though Father Abraham himself in reality flourished rather later than the Thirty Years' War (1642-1709). The art with which Schiller has contrived to compress into a hundred lines, or little more, every characteristic trait of the original, the homely wit and Teutonic humour, the mixture of shrewdness and absurdity, the plain speaking interwoven with scriptural symbolism, marks the sermon as the highest example of his command over comedy. This was the kind of appeal that touched the consciences of disbanded soldiers, and woeful village congregations, among the unspeakable horrors of the seventeenth century in Germany. When the Friar turns from his picture of the Empire to abuse the army for its sins, how absurd is the inconsequence of his illustration; yet, but for the rhyme, the whole passage might have been taken word for word from one of the Jesuit's tracts :—

> "*Ubi erit victoriæ spes,
> Si offenditur Deus?* How can we win,
> If you shirk the sermon and services,
> And do nothing all day but lie in an inn?
> The woman, as the gospels tell,
> Found the penny she sought so well;
> His father's asses were found by Saul;
> Joseph's sweet brothers—he found them all;
> But find fear of God in a soldier crew,
> Or decent behaviour or modest shame,
> Why! a man might look till all was blue,
> Though he sought with a hundred lamps aflame."

Turning for a new text to the words of the Baptist spoken to the soldiers in the wilderness, he adapts the old advice freely to modern requirements. He next deals with breaches of the third commandment, reminding them that, though Joshua was a good soldier, and David slew Goliath, it is not written that either of them cursed and swore; and, after some similar exhortations against stealing, he suddenly breaks off, and with rising passion and greater solemnity of tone, he turns to hint at the source from which all these offences come:

> "But to blame the servants is waste of power,
> When the sin must lie at a higher door;
> The limbs but follow the Head's commands;
> On whom *he* believes, none understands."

As long as he had been denouncing themselves alone and the army in general, the soldiers had listened with the amused interest usually displayed by congregations under their minister's rebuke, each mentally shifting the burden of blame on to his neighbour; but the moment that he ventures a word against their General, an outcry is heard, the confusion and tumult is renewed, and he continues to blurt out his denunciations amidst constant interruptions and threatenings that at last drive-him, discomfited, but still eloquently punning, from the scene, protected from actual violence in his retreat only by the consideration of two Croats. When he is gone, and the simple peasant who has been detected with his loaded dice has narrowly escaped hanging, and been driven home again to some slower form of ruin, the conversation becomes graver and more serious. The news has come that the army is to be gradually broken up, and that some of the troops have been already detached from Wallenstein under the pretext of an escort to Flanders. They recount again the story of the army's formation and greatness; their minds are full of suspicions, but having sworn to stand by the general whatever may betide, they attempt to renew their former careless gaiety with the song, "Up, comrades, away, to horse, to horse!" And with this ringing chorus, in praise of the soldier's life, the scene closes.

The serio-comic representation of *Wallenstein's Camp* is followed by *The Piccolomini*, a drama in five acts, certainly the least satisfactory part of the whole tragedy. Schiller should have been guided by the wisdom of his own saying—

"Other masters are judged by what they've wisely expressed;
By what he wisely omits the master of style is confessed."

With more self-denying courage, the whole of *The*

Piccolomini, as it now stands, might have been omitted. It is unnecessary, or might easily be rendered unnecessary by a few alterations in the final tragedy, which would itself gain considerably by the change and compression. If it were a new piece, no modern theatrical manager would venture to put it on the stage, though that, of course, cannot fairly be urged in its disfavour, for the same would no doubt be true of most of the Shaksperian dramas as well as of all Schiller's. At all events, it may help us to sympathise with Goethe's regret in old age, that, though he could still read many scenes from Schiller's works with great interest, he often had to give up the effort, because the idea seemed forced and unnatural. *The Piccolomini*, in fact, can only be regarded as a kind of interlude, in which the situation leading up to the final tragedy is further-explained. Its effect is too much like the long introductory speeches in some Euripidean tragedies. In itself it contains little action or dramatic interest, and it results only in explanations that might almost as well be inserted as notes to the list of *dramatis personæ* on the play-bill. We learn from it that the jealousies which at the Diet of Ratisbon, some four years before, had removed Wallenstein from command of the Imperial army, but had of grudging necessity disappeared when it was found that his genius alone could foil Gustavus Adolphus and his Swedes, had been gradually recovering strength since the day of Lützen, and were now omnipotent at the Court. The Emperor's deputy has just arrived at Pilsen to investigate the

---

* In the earlier editions, followed by Coleridge in his translation, *The Piccolomini* was continued to the end of what is now the second act in *Wallenstein's Death*.

charges against Wallenstein. He already holds the warrant for his degradation. Octavio Piccolomini, the intimate friend and subordinate officer of the general, has been appointed his successor; but the orders are still secret. Meantime we learn that the suspicions of Wallenstein's treachery are no longer unfounded. Though he still hesitates, he is actually intriguing with the Swedes and the leaders of the Protestant cause. To be ready for the decisive step, he has collected the army and summoned his officers to Pilsen; has even sent the favoured and distinguished young soldier, Max Piccolomini, Octavio's son, of whom we have heard words of high praise from the soldiers in the camp, to conduct the Duchess and their daughter Thekla to the same place of safety. His intention is already known to some of the assembled officers, and, realising the necessity of immediate and concerted action, though ignorant how close the danger has actually approached, they prepare a declaration binding themselves to Wallenstein and his cause, whatever it may be, and, by a trick at a banquet, induce most of their colleagues to sign it. Max, almost alone, refuses to sign till the purport be further explained. The scene is the most animated in this part of the play, but it is in reality little more than an episode, for it only serves to increase the sense of suspicion and intrigue, and to intensify the struggle in Max's mind between affection and duty which forms the subordinate plot in the drama. After the banquet, his father, Octavio, reveals to him Wallenstein's intended treachery, and commands him to remain true to his allegiance to the Emperor, and forsake his old friend and patron, whose daughter, Thekla, he has just learnt to love. He refuses to believe the story, but his father's words are confirmed by the capture of a messenger with despatches from Wallenstein to the Swedes. As he rushes wildly away to demand the truth from the general himself, the drama suddenly breaks off. It will be evident that *The Piccolomini* is not a play of any kind, but merely an introduction to a play, a statement of the situation. As such, it met with inevitable failure on the stage. Jean Paul, who was present at the first performance, wrote of it as follows:—"It is excellent—rather tedious—and false. We have beautiful language, strong poetic passages, some good scenes, no character, no stream of action, and no conclusion." No criticism could be more complete.

The subordinate plot, which tells the story of Max and Thekla, their loves, their virtue, and their fate, does not reach its consummation till the end of the fourth act in *Wallenstein's Death*. It is the idealist's protest against the spirit of intrigue and mundane ambition prevailing in the rest of the drama. Schiller introduced it to give sweetness and dignity to an action that he feared would otherwise fail to win the sympathy of the audience. He was perhaps wrong, for the fall of greatness through its own error has often been proved to be strong enough in itself to stir the depths of emotion; but it is hard to regret a mistake to which we owe the creation of two figures that have been so inspiring to the youth of Germany, and not of Germany alone. In Max and Thekla Schiller had subjects such as he delighted to depict, conceptions on which he might lavish all the wealth of imagined perfection. Max is a fearless young officer, a hero to his men, who are ready to die with him in any mad enterprise; yet he is gentle as a woman, and pours out lyrical raptures in praise of peace. He meets us in the first transport of requited love, when all seems clear and bright before him. He is fighting for the Emperor and the true cause, under the general whom he has served and worshipped from boyhood, and now that general's daughter has deigned to illumine his life with the peaceful moonbeams of her love. Noble-hearted, clear of insight, swift and immovable in decision, unhesitating in her high sense of duty, incapable of fear when the supreme crisis of peril comes, she too has for a moment ventured to be happy. on leaving her convent walls. But the clouds gather quickly. Thekla perceives that her love is being used by her mother's sister, the Countess Terzky, only as a means of binding Max and his followers irrevocably to Wallenstein's cause. Max learns that his trusted benefactor is meditating an alliance with Swedes and Protestants, which to his frank and open nature is simply treachery, under whatever other names it may be disguised. In vain he implores Wallenstein to his face to return to his allegiance or even to declare open war. By his refusal the doom of the lovers is sealed. In an atmosphere of treason and intrigue those innocent and chivalrous souls cannot breathe. For one moment, it is true, love makes the young man reel from his course; it was hard to surrender that bright and short-lived vision of joy, just when all had seemed so sure and fair. But Thekla has no doubts; with a woman's happy limitation she sees all things plain, and by her strength his own is renewed. Only one way now remains for him; he cannot betray the emperor, neither can he range himself against his general, the father of his bride. Calling his devoted troopers round him, he dashes out against a strong position of the Swedes, and is the first to find the honoured death he seeks. His followers are cut down to a man. At Eger, whither she has gone from Pilsen with her father, Thekla hears from a Swedish soldier the story of the end. Having rid herself of the troublesome advice of the Countess Terzky, and the feeble lamentations of her mother, she listens with forced calmness till the last detail is told. Her plan is already fixed; she will die on his grave. She courteously dismisses the soldier; "Now let me go," she says to her waiting-woman. "Where should we go?" the waiting-woman asks. "There is but one place," she answers:

"There is but one place in creation's round."

She has no fear nor hesitation. The lady suggests the discomforts of the way, the dangers from the Swedes and insolent soldiers. "Was *his* bed soft," she answers, "beneath the horses' hoofs?" and again:

"Unhappinesss goes free from pole to pole.

It will be evident that, beautiful as these two figures have generally been acknowledged to be, whatever opinion may have prevailed as to the propriety of their introduction into the drama at all, they are in reality types rather than actual characters; and as such they are representative of Schiller's favourite creations. He delighted in noble and inspiring types that sometimes remind us rather strangely of Scott's heroes and heroines, having the same virtues of dignity, courtesy, purity, and fearlessness, and the same weakness of unreality. But whereas in Scott we have only to turn from his heroes to his peasants, fools, and vagabonds, and we pass from a world of types to the world of life, in Schiller we seldom find this contrast, for he had a different conception of what is required from the creative mind. To him unreality of a certain kind would have seemed no offence, but rather a point to be attained. Whether rightly or wrongly, to him, at all events, the poetic world was distinct from the actual, and came under different laws. He made no effort to deceive the spectator by representation of life, but purposely avoided it rather, using, with this special object, a regular metre, language unlike the talk of every day, and those long and sometimes lyrical speeches that would seem so strange and wearisome to a modern audience. Partly for this reason also, partly because he fell short of the highest creative genius, the characters in his plays appear as typical embodiments of virtues and vices rather than living men and women, and hence, in an unimaginative and intensely realistic age like our own, they are only sure of sympathy from childhood and impetuous youth, to which the elements of life are still simple, the lines of conduct absolutely sure, and the region of imagination wide.

If we turn from the episodes, too long and numerous for dramatic art, we find in the fall of Wallenstein a central theme worthy of tragedy. We contemplate the ruin of a hero and his house consummated by fate and his own blind but deliberate error. During the first division of the drama he does not appear upon the stage, and in the second he appears but seldom.

But by rumours of his greatness and the mystery that surrounds him, our minds are gradually rendered expectant, all the more because he holds aloof:

> "Like to a lonely dragon, that his fen
> Makes fear'd, and talked of more than seen."*

When he first appears, though he has already inclined to the evil, the choice of the good is still open to him. It would still be possible to resign without dishonour, or even, as he thinks, to remain in his office and allegiance. But, on the other hand, he longs to requite the insults of the jealous nobility, and to grasp for his own the crown of Bohemia, the source of these long troubles. And his aim is not entirely selfish. He is full of a higher patriotism than fidelity to an emperor. He remembers with anguish the sufferings that he has himself inflicted at the Emperor's word upon the unhappy German people. Peacefully to deliver Germany from the stranger, to save her from armies that for years had made her a prey, could hardly be called treason. And yet he shrinks from the final step. He remembers the Emperor's favours to him in earlier days; he thinks of the universal contempt that awaits a traitor. He would still draw back if he were able, for he surely never meant to go so far. More had been said than he could now stand to:—

> "Bold was the word, because the deed was coward."

And now he doubts his purpose: hither and thither he casts his restless mind, and the hags of hesitation and uncertainty rend the sinews of his will. Since that day

* *Coriolanus*, Act iv., Sc. 1.

of degradation at Ratisbon he has not been the man he was. The cheerful confidence of earlier life has gone, and its place is taken by a gloomy fatalism that gropes in darkness, listening to shadowy warnings, and prying into the courses of the stars. For counsel he turns to a solemn fool of an astrologer, as Saul to the witch of Endor, Lysander to the shrine of Ammon, and Macbeth to the Weird Sisters. He has no trust in himself, nor much hope for the success of treason, if treason there must be; though it is not force he fears, but custom, the most ancient of the gods. " Power," he says—

> " Power seated on a quiet throne thou'dst shake,
> Power on an ancient consecrated throne,
> Strong in possession, founded in old custom :
> Power by a thousand tough and stringy roots
> Fixed to the people's pious nursery-faith.
> . . . . 'Tis a foe invisible,
> The which I fear—a fearful enemy,
> Which in the human heart opposes me,
> By its coward fear alone made fearful to me.
> Not that, which, full of life, instinct with power,
> Makes known its present being, that is not
> The true, the perilously formidable.
> O, no ! it is the common, the quite common,
> The thing of an eternal yesterday,
> Which ever was, and evermore returns,
> Sterling to-morrow, for to-day 'twas sterling!
> For of the wholly common is man made,
> And custom is his nurse ! Woe then to them,
> Who lay irreverent hands upon his old
> House-furniture, the dear inheritance
> From his forefathers. For time consecrates ;
> And what is grey with age becomes religion."*

* This, together with most of the subsequent extracts from *Wallenstein's Death*, is from Coleridge's celebrated translation.

He tries to shift the blame of his weakness and delay onto the inscrutable powers of destiny, not knowing the truth of Napoleon's saying to Goethe, "Fate? Politics are fate." He finds his only solace in consulting maps of the heavens, and the signs and wonders of astrological lore. Mystery fills him with a fearful delight:—

> "Not without shudder does a mortal hand
> Grope in the secret urn of destiny."

In vain the generals who share his purposed treason implore him to act with decision before it be too late, entreating him "to seek his star of fate in his own breast." In vain they warn him of Octavio's treachery. The stars, he answers, are not ready; the stars assure him Piccolomini must be true. It seems as though nothing can rouse him from the apparent lethargy of tormenting hesitation. Not even the taunts of his wife's sister, Countess Terzky, can prevail, though she draws this picture of the alternative to treason:—*

> "I see how all will end. The King of Hungary
> Makes his appearance, and 'twill of itself
> Be understood, that then the Duke retires.
>
> There will not want a formal declaration.
> The young King will administer the oath
> To the whole army; and so all returns
> To the old position. On some morrow morning
> The Duke departs; and now 'tis stir and bustle
> Within his castles. He will hunt, and build,
> Superintend his horses' pedigrees;
> Creates himself a court, gives golden keys,

* The King of Hungary, of whom she speaks, is the Emperor's nominee to the crown of Bohemia; the Duke is, of course, Wallenstein himself, Duke of Friedland.

> And introduceth strictest ceremony
> In fine proportions, and nice etiquette ;
> Keeps open table with high cheer ; in brief,
> Commenceth mighty king—in miniature."

But the hesitation, which neither entreaty nor scorn can resolve, vanishes as danger gathers round him.

> "It must be night ere Friedland's star can shine."

Tidings of disaster come quickly in, like the messengers to Job. His papers are captured; his negotiations with the Swede laid bare ; most of his generals desert in horror at the thought of treason ; some of his soldiers even fall away. Prague is lost, the centre of his position, the capital of his hoped-for kingdom. Worse than all, he hears of the treachery of Octavio Piccolomini, the man whom he had trusted in spite of all warnings, who had been his comrade from the first. The blow is hard, for he has strong natural affections, and Octavio's son is his own favourite, and his daughter's lover.

> "'The wildest savage,' he cries, 'drinks not with the victim
> Into whose breast he means to plunge the sword.'"

And leaning on the shoulder of Butler, another trusted veteran, he laments the days of friendship now proved false—

> "Thirty years have we together
> Lived out, and held out, sharing joy and hardship.
> We have slept in one camp-bed, drunk from one glass,
> Our morsel shared ! I leaned myself on *him*,
> As now I lean me on *thy* faithful shoulder."

And all the time, like Duncan in *Macbeth*, he is turning for solace from treachery to a darker traitor, and the man on whose shoulder he leans is already plotting his destruction for some fancied slight of years gone by. But for Wallenstein the worst is now over; disaster has made his course plain, and courage and cheerful decision return. Schiller himself is reported once to have said, "The only real misery in life is fear;" and when hesitation ends, the worst part of fear is over.

Leaving Pilsen with his family, and the regiments and generals still true to him, he advances rapidly to Eger, where on the morrow he is to effect a junction with the Swedes, and surrender the town into their hands. Though fallen, he is still strong, for he has the attraction of genius and great personality. Butler, watching at his side, knows that the time is short, and determines to end the matter that very night. By representing Wallenstein's undoubted treason against the Emperor, he wins a grudging accomplice in Gordon, the warden of the castle. Baser murderers are also won. The other officers he puts to death at a banquet late in the evening, and then turns to the remote part of the castle where Wallenstein's silent chambers are placed. The Duke himself has despatched the last message to the Swedes, and all is ready for the morrow. When the need for action is over, something of the former gloom returns; he too cannot escape the power of the "eternal yesterday," and the ties to the past of a glorious life are not lightly rent. He grieves also for the death of Max, and for his daughter's sorrow. The Countess Terzky is with him, and she too is disturbed by dreams and omens. Turning to the window he looks out upon the night—

> " There is a busy motion in the heaven,
> The wind doth chase the flag upon the tower,
> Fast sweep the clouds, the sickle of the moon,
> Struggling, darts snatches of uncertain light.
> No form of star is visible! That one
> White stain of light, that single glimmering yonder,
> Is from Cassiopeia, and therein
> Is Jupiter. (*A pause.*) But now
> The blackness of the troubled element hides him.
>
> [*He sinks into profound melancholy, and looks vacantly into the distance.*]
>
> *Countess.* What art thou brooding on?
>
> *Wal.*   Methinks,
> If I but saw him, 'twould be well with me.
> He is the star of my nativity,
> And often marvellously hath his aspect
> Shot strength into my heart."

Soon afterwards she goes, sick with vague apprehension. Gordon brings report of the quiet of the town, and they talk together over old times when they were young. Gordon does his best to warn, and to dissuade him from his purpose. The astrologer hastens in and joins his entreaties, for the stars are adverse and foretell the near approach of some overwhelming woe. The groom, who has been assisting him to disrobe, falls at his feet in mute supplication. But Wallenstein's confidence has returned; the future again seems full of hope; he laughs at their fears, and as he retires to his inner room, he carelessly utters the bodeful words—

> "Gordon, good night! I think to make a long
> Sleep of it: for the struggle and the turmoil
> Of this last day or two were great. May't please you !
> Take care that they awake me not too early."

Already Butler and the murderers are at hand. Gordon implores in vain for mercy, for one hour's delay. A trumpet is heard in the distance. He is thrust aside. The groom is killed, and the murderers force their way into Wallenstein's chamber. When all is over, the Countess is seen anxiously returning, for she has found that Thekla has fled. She is met by the cries of murder. In the midst of the confusion, Octavio Piccolomini enters with his train as the representative of the Emperor. At the sight of Wallenstein's dead body, which is carried over the back of the stage, he deplores the rash event. Turning from reproof of Butler, he meets the Countess, who for a moment had disappeared, and now has drunk poison. In dying accents she thus delivers to him the story of the doom of Wallenstein and his house—

> "These are the fruits
> Of your contrivances. The Duke is dead,
> My husband too is dead, the Duchess struggles
> In the pangs of death, my niece has disappeared.
> This house of splendour and of princely glory
> Doth now stand desolated : the affrighted servants
> Rush forth through all its doors. I am the last
> Therein ; I shut it up, and here deliver
> The keys of it."

At the first performance of *Wallenstein's Death* at Weimar, the effect is described as having been overwhelming. The whole theatre sobbed. The actors were overcome with tears, and could not continue their parts. It is true that the nation and the times were lachrymose. But Goethe, writing of it soberly to Humboldt afterwards, described it as springing up from the two introductory plays like a miraculous flower from the sepal; and in spite of the faults evident enough to every critic, it remains one of the very few great tragedies of modern times.

Apart from technicalities of theatrical representation, and a few minor blemishes from which we can see that Schiller, like so many dramatists, allowed himself to be hampered in his art by the traditions of history, the most serious charge that can be brought against the drama is the presence of an uncomfortable suspicion that Wallenstein's own character is not quite strong enough for the part. He hardly satisfies our expectation; and it is probably unfortunate that he is introduced in an agony of hesitation, the sin that heaven and earth find it hardest to forgive, especially in a soldier. And yet Macbeth hesitates, and does not altogether lose our sympathy, nor even our admiration. But Wallenstein has not the poetic imagination of Macbeth, and does not win our pity over the perversion and ruin of a consummate intellect. When his resolve is taken, we have a sense of relief and not of horror, though it is taken for evil; for we feel that now admiration and pity may be possible. And yet our hopes are never quite fulfilled; perhaps he is too conscious of his guilt, and makes too much excuse for his treason. The odium of treachery clings to him, almost as much as to the self-righteous Octavio. There is something wanting in the man. Coriolanus goes over to the enemy, but no one thinks of Coriolanus as a traitor; for we are borne away by the strength and magnificence of the character. It is certain that Schiller was himself conscious of the weak point, but unfortunately thought himself compelled to follow history in a matter so familiar to all his audience.

A Greek dramatist derived his subject from traditions handed down in fit poetic form by generations of poets; but Schiller had to piece out the rough jottings of prosaic chroniclers. Consequently, he was never fully satisfied with his representation of his hero's character, and tried rather to detract attention from it by episodes and similar devices. Nevertheless, in the movement and terror of the closing scenes, and in the grand conception of the whole drama, involving the future and the doom of armies, peoples, and religions, we lose sight of the minor weaknesses of construction and character, and realise only that we are contemplating a vast action of complex human force, moving us by error and disaster to pity and fear, and fulfilling the high demand of tragedy, as for three centuries it has seldom been fulfilled.

Exhausted as he had been at the completion of the drama, so that he writes in March 1799 as though weary of life, and thinking nothing more worth living for, yet, on the very day after the first performance of *Wallenstein's Death*, Schiller began to prepare the scheme for his next tragedy by studying the chronicles of Mary Queen of Scots. During the summer and autumn, however, he was much interrupted, and made little progress. The King of Prussia, with his beautiful wife, the parents of the Emperor William I., came to Weimar, and demanded a special performance of *Wallenstein*. Goethe and he were also occupied with the analysis of Dilettantism. Other dramatic projects distracted his attention, especially the story of Warbeck, and an adaptation of *Macbeth* for the German stage. He began negotiations with the Grand

Duke for a removal to Weimar, that he might be nearer the theatre. And in the end his wife fell dangerously ill of fever and mental derangement after the birth of their third child. Nevertheless, besides the completion of *Wallenstein*, this year saw the production of Schiller's most celebrated, if not his greatest lyric, the *Song of the Bell*. The idea was perhaps derived from a bell-foundry near Volkstädt which he used to visit in his early days of courtship eleven years before, and there is at least one mention of it in the interim (1797). Otherwise we know little or nothing of its history, except that it was finished in the early autumn of 1799 for the *Muses' Almanack* of the following year—the last number of that annual—and that the beautiful motto (*Vivos voco. Mortuos plango. Fulgura frango*) was taken from the old bell in Schaffhausen Minster, of which Schiller found an account in some treatise on bell-casting.

For the form of the *Song of the Bell* it would perhaps be hard to find an exact parallel in English literature, unless we went to some imitator of Schiller, such as Longfellow. It is written in an irregular rhyming metre, and extends to something over four hundred short lines, the whole tone being lyric and ideal, so that it is entirely different in character from the narrative poetry and realistic pictures of such works as the *Parish Register* or the *Task*. It consists of descriptions of various phases of human life, suggested in symbol to the poet by the various processes of casting a church bell; partly, also, by the varied functions of the bell when complete. The smelting and purifying of the metal suggest the years of childhood and youth.* The testing of the metal, to try how the component parts will fuse and bind together under the stress of fire, naturally finds its parallel in the discipline of marriage. There follow other pictures of simple human joys and disaster, the outbreak of fire, and the destruction of the home; the death of the wife and mother; the peace of summer evening in a well-ordered and contented state contrasted with the terrors of revolution, when, as it were, the metal, still hot and liquid, has burst the cast and the molten streams run over into shapeless chaos. At last the bell is finished; Concordia is its name; it is swung into its place above the houses of men to proclaim the common sympathy of mankind in joy and sorrow; its first note shall be peace.

There are, perhaps, in all languages, certain poems that have gone to the heart of the people more deeply than their actual poetic worth would seem to justify. It is not merely that they have a vogue for a time like a popular song or a novel; they retain a hold on each generation and become part of the people's common inheritance. The critics may sneer, but they are roughly reminded that, until quite recently at all events, poetry was not written for the critics. And

* It is an instance of Schiller's want of carefulness in thought that he here describes the years of childhood as "fleeting swift as an arrow." If there could be one commonplace more universally acknowledged than another, it would surely be that of Campbell's verse,

"The more we live, more brief appear
Our life's succeeding stages;
A day to childhood seems a year,
And years like passing ages."

so with the *Song of the Bell*. The Schlegels and the Romantic School down to the last and greatest of them, "the Romanticist unfrocked," might shriek with scornful laughter; the modern critic may pour contempt upon its "Philistinism," may call its ideals the virtues and comforts of a bourgeois housewife, may jest at this Dutch delight in cupboards, linen, and stores, at the cheerful optimism of unvarying work, uneventful marriage, and a peaceful hope of family life beyond the grave. It makes no difference. The German people listens, and goes on learning the poem by heart. In these lines the poet has gathered up ideals of existence that still appeal most profoundly to the race in spite of every change. He has depicted with poetic elevation the kind of life still most dear to the average healthy-minded German, with his sober love of wife and child and household stuff, of ordered freedom and benevolent Fatherland; and having thus laid, as it were, a sanction upon it, he has succeeded in creating a truly national poem. He has done for the life of the German people, as a whole, what Milton in his earlier poems did for the life of the scholar.

In December 1799 the Schiller family was at last able to remove to Weimar, the Grand-Duke having promised a pension of £30 a-year, which was afterwards more than doubled. They thus welcomed-in the new century in a new home; but the well-known Schiller-house on the Esplanade, now called the Schiller Strasse, was not procured till 1802, when it was purchased for about £700 from Mr. Mellish, an Englishman, the translator of *Maria Stuart*, and an intimate friend of both Schiller and Goethe. Weimar now continued to be Schiller's home for the remaining few years of his life, though he would at intervals return to Jena for short visits in search of peace and quiet after the wearisome gossip and petty convulsions of Weimar society, in which, as he said, there was very little intellect in circulation, but any amount of idle people craving for nervous excitement. And since to the dilettante mind no nervous excitement is so stimulating as artistic jealousy and scandal, the pellucid surface of that refined society was continually ruffled by storms, which, during quarrels between rival actresses, often rose to hurricanes. And all the time, just across the low line of hills, their nation was falling to ruin, and the enemy was advancing from victory to victory into the heart of the land; whilst, further away, the First Consul was already crossing the Alps as the next step to the subjugation of Europe. On the very day when the bosom of Weimar was rent in furious faction over the first performance of *Maria Stuart*, Marengo was being fought. But the doom that awaits national apathy was to be deferred for six years yet.

CHAPTER VII.

WHATEVER judgment we may pass on the blind pursuit of a thin and languid form of culture in Weimar society, it is certain that to Schiller, himself the change was very welcome after Jena, where he had complained that the atmosphere of learning and metaphysics stifled his creative power. And the result justified his expectation of increased mental vigour, for, in spite of aggravated ill-health which at times reduced him to impotent misery for weeks together, the five an ! a-half years of life that were left him, after the removal to Weimar, were marked by the production of four great dramas and the beginning of a fifth, not to speak of numerous adaptations of French and other plays for the German stage. The time was indeed almost entirely divided between the labour of composition and the relaxation of illness, so that there remains but little biographical incident to record.

On the broad and thickly-wooded hill of the Ettersberg, that rises some two or three miles north-west of Weimar, like a solitary wave from the open plain with its long strips of cultivated land, there stood one of the grand-ducal lodges or country-seats—palaces by courtesy—such as are frequent throughout the little realm, and reveal so pathetic an admixture of grotesque magnificence and beautiful simplicity. When the life of Weimar was younger, the Ettersburg had been the frequent scene of poetic revels, and here, in the Spring of 1800, Schiller retired that he might finish his tragedy of *Maria Stuart* among the silent forests of fir and beech. It was performed for the first time on June 14, in the Weimar theatre, with due ceremony, but the critical public was much divided as to its merits. Punctual housewives especially complained that the speeches were too long, and that the curtain did not fall till ten o'clock. One lady, who seems to have been the leader of an opposition party to Schiller, remarked that it was no wonder people thought him a great tragedian when he had the power of torturing them so. And yet, though it contains nothing so noble as certain passages in *Wallenstein*, and though the conception does not, as a whole, attain to the same grandeur and breadth of interest, it marks a distinct advance in Schiller's dramatic art. It displays far greater control over the subject, and a ripened experience of the stage and its necessities. The purpose is more coherent, and the plot elaborated with greater skill than perhaps in any other of Schiller's plays; and it was probably the art of its construction that made Madame de Staël, who was likely to be an exact judge in such matters, call it the best-conceived, as well as the most pathetic, of German tragedies. Except in the anti-climax of compelling the audience to return to Elizabeth and her court after they have listened to the thud of the axe which tells that all is over, hardly a dramatic error can be detected in the arrangement of any scene. The situations are strong, and the characters, for Schiller, complex but distinct. The reputation of the play, however, is due rather to its pathos than to the art of its construction. The opportunities offered to an actress of genius by Queen Mary's wild outburst of joy in her brief glimpse of the sky, the clouds, the water, and all things free, by the mingled dignity and passion of her defiance to her rival and persecutor in their subsequent meeting, and by the tenderness of her farewells, as she is led to the scaffold, have made it one of the stock pieces of the German theatre, and secured it success on the English stage, even in recent years. In the plot Schiller has followed history, as far as he could know it, more closely than is usual with him. The action begins with Mary's condemnation, and closes with her execution and the wild efforts of Elizabeth to shirk responsibility for the deed; the scene is laid for the most part at Fotheringay, which Schiller seems to have supposed to be in the near neighbourhood of the London Court. Nearly all the characters are historic, and are not much distorted from the truth. In Mortimer we have but an imagined type of those many impassioned and chivalrous youths whose devotion, through torture and doom, to their afflicted Queen of Beauty, gives a mournful grandeur to her words as she waits for death:

"Much hatred have I known, and much love too."

In the characters of the two queens themselves, Schiller was no doubt led into some exaggeration by what he considered the necessities of the drama; but it may be noticed that his portrait of Elizabeth fails rather from omission of her good qualities than from insistence on her bad. And if we are inclined to think that his Queen Mary comes too near the lamentable heroine of girlish romance, we must remember that other poets and greater historians than Schiller have failed to fill in the astonishing outline of the contemporary records, and to exhaust the mystery of that soul at whose creation Nature said, "I will make a *woman* of my own."

In the *Maid of Orleans*, which was begun immediately after *Maria Stuart*, and was finished in April 1801, Schiller had again to deal with a subject the tragedy of which no poetic invention can heighten; and in this case, therefore, his success was proportionately less the further he allowed himself to depart from history. Some critics have urged that it is mere pedantry to object to his deliberate perversion of truth, when his sole object was the improvement of his work as art. If art had gained by the perversion, there would indeed have been no more to be said. But it may be answered that the objection is not to his inaccuracy as a historian, but to his error as a poet in supposing that for the sake of art it was possible thus to improve on the truth of such a history as this. Truth tells of a poor little peasant-girl, "une pauvre petite bergerette," not beautiful in face, but simple and honest of look, in figure short and square, the black hair close cropped, the gown of rough red frieze—who, with unquestioning trust in her saints, her banner, and her sword, saves her country at its uttermost need, when all had given it over, and its rulers were contending over its dying body. Her belief converts the relaxed and mutinous rabble of panic-stricken armies into bands of heroes. Her devotion breathes the air of life upon a stagnant age when faith seemed dead. We see her working all things, enduring all things, wounded, confident, triumphant. And then comes the story of the end, her sacrifice to the spite and jealousies of the idle court she had saved, the bargain for her life, the trial where the representatives of God declare her faith to be of the devil, the shameful sufferings of the prison, the pitiless death, the ashes scattered in the river. Every element of the profoundest tragedy is there, and all that art could hope to do would be to read the truth aright. And yet Schiller has been applauded for presenting us with an idealised maid, with flowing hair and majestic mien, the fairest and most gifted in the country-side, one who wins by eloquence and supernatural signs, who debates and analyses like a modern heroine, who, like a novel-bred girl, falls in love at first sight, and becomes self-conscious and melancholy, who is uncertain of her motives, who has not the courage to declare her innocence, but impotently surrenders to what she calls fate, who, finally, that the feelings of the audience may not be lacerated beyond all comfort, bursts her chains by miraculous aid, and gloriously dies in the arms of victory upon the ensanguined field. It is not because historic truth has been violated that others besides the mere pedant will protest against such treatment of the story; it is because the real essence of the tragedy has been lost. It is significant that the late Professor Scherer, the best recent critic of German literature, detects something operatic in the whole of this drama; and indeed it would be easy to recast it as a libretto for Italian opera in the old style, with arias and duos, and the Maid as *prima donna*.

And yet, though owing to the general familiarity and incomparably higher grandeur of the historic narrative, the play must be regarded as a failure, it displays, in some degree, the characteristics of all Schiller's later dramas—elevation of language, careful arrangement, strong theatrical situations. The minor characters also are elaborated with unusual attention. The King reminds us of Henry VI., or even Richard II.; and few passages in Schiller are so Shakspearian as the dying utterances of Talbot. An imitation of some of the lines may here be permitted, if only to show a quotation, long since hackneyed, in its original context. The English army has been defeated by the maid, Talbot is severely wounded, and at the news that Paris has fallen as well as Rheims, he tears the bandages from his wounds and gives himself up to death.

> " Folly, the game is thine, and I am spent.
> Against stupidity the gods themselves
> Take arms in vain. O wisdom, heavenly light,
> Daughter of God's high head, wise builder up
> Of the ancient universe, of stars the guide,
> Where art thou then, now that to the mad horse
> Of foolishness thou in thy pride art bound,
> And, vainly shrieking, with thy drunken mate
> Art hurl'd, eyes open, down to the abyss?
> Accursed is he who steers his little life
> Toward greatness and the good, and with wise chart
> Maps out his careful course. The king of fools
> In motley rules the world."

Owing to local difficulties, the *Maid of Orleans* did not first appear on the Weimar stage, the notorious position of the leading actress too obviously unfitting her for the part. The Grand Duke also considered the whole thing too risky a venture to be tried before an audience that knew Voltaire's *Pucelle* almost by heart; so deeply does burlesque corrupt by its associations. But in other centres of dramatic art, especially in Berlin, it appears to have been performed with remarkable success, and to the half-educated men and women that generally compose the mass of a theatrical audience it is undoubtedly the most exciting and effective of all Schiller's later plays.

An incident that occurred at Leipzig in the September after the completion of the drama affords remarkable evidence of its popularity and of Schiller's growing fame. He was returning from Dresden, where he had been paying a long and, as it turned out, a last visit to his early friends, the Körners, who had given up their dwelling in the vineyard outside the town to him and his family. In passing through Leipzig he was present at a performance of the *Maid of Orleans* given in his honour. When he appeared in the box the whole audience rose and greeted him with tumultuous cheering. The piece was played amid continual applause, and at the end the streets along which the poet was to pass to his hotel were lined with enthusiastic crowds.

On his return home Schiller devoted himself with renewed energy to the Weimar theatre, in the management of which he had practically become Goethe's partner. Besides the composition and adaptation of new pieces for the boards, he superintended the minor details of performances, and especially the training of the actors. "Like myself," said Goethe to Eckermann, "Schiller associated constantly with the actors and actresses, and was always present at rehearsals." In the correspondence between the two friends we find frequent reference to the ignorance and stupidity against which they had to contend in preparing a new drama. Even during the performance the actors would speak as though no audience was present, and were either commonplace or exaggerated, the result being that the spectators, who were attentive, but in the main uneducated, only applauded ranting. Schiller bitterly complained that his verse was uttered in the natural and conversational tone of everyday life, whereas he desired blank-verse to be treated as an entirely ideal mode of expression, and it was his declared object, as an artist, "to wage eternal war against all Naturalism." The managers further encountered a similar difficulty in the choice of the dramas themselves. Goethe was determined, at all costs, to elevate the stage, and with this object he despotically imposed upon the audience all manner of unpopular pieces which he considered best suited to improve their taste. He himself translated Voltaire's *Mahomet*, partly, it is true, to please the Grand Duke, who always had a hankering after the French drama. Schiller adapted Gozzi's *Turandot*, and, at a later time, *Phèdre-Nathan the Wise*, and some plays of Terence were also put on the stage. If the public ventured to protest against this compulsory education in taste, they were summarily silenced. In one particularly trying case, Goethe from his box had to command them not to laugh, and they instantly obeyed. But such scenes were not likely to increase the popularity of the management, and though, for the most part, the citizens were awed into submission by Goethe's immense reputation, an occasional rebellious outburst, which fluttered society for a month or more, proved that in this, as in other instances, the attempt to raise the vulgar taste by any shorter method than nature's own slow course, was, after all, a failure. For the road to beauty is royal, and the vulgar must become kings before they can enter on it.

Perhaps the most notorious of their rebellious outbursts is connected with the name of Kotzebue, whose satiric dramas and light comedies were most popular with the German public, and were received with favour even in England and on other foreign stages. Returning to his native Weimar after a wandering life in the Austrian and Russian capitals, and a period of exile in Siberia, he had obtained considerable honour in his own country, and now, as Goethe steadily persisted in cutting out all his smartest contemporary allusions, and would not produce more than a certain proportion of his innumberable plays, he determined that it was time the despot of the stage was deposed. His mode of action was worthy of the man who was afterwards to fall a victim to the assassin for his traitorous intrigues. The first step was, if possible, to isolate Goethe by alienating him from Schiller; and with this object he followed the golden rule that praise of one friend rather than the other will dissolve the strongest friendship. Having organised a little band of spiteful ladies and other malcontents for the special worship of Schiller, he proposed in March 1802 to hold a ceremonial function in his honour in the town-hall. The *Song of the Bell* was to be recited, and, as a climax to the performance, Kotzebue was to break a huge model of a bell on the platform, and reveal a bust of Schiller being crowned

SCHILLER. 165

by a Genius. The poet himself, much against his will, was forced to promise to be present at his own apotheosis. But, fortunately, despotism reigned in other departments than the theatre; on the festal day the authorities refused the use both of bust and hall, and the intriguing enthusiasts withdrew discomfited to their cave. In the following month Schiller removed to his new and final home on the Esplanade, within three minutes' walk of the theatre. In the same year the Grand Duke purchased for him from the Imperial Court the title of *von*, which admitted him unquestioned to the privilege of Court society. Like other distinguished friends of liberty who took the title, the Schillers protested they only did it for the sake of their children; but at the same time the poet admitted that in a little place like Weimar it was well not to be excluded from anything.

Schiller's next drama, the *Bride of Messina*, which was completed in February 1803, and acted at Weimar in the following month, was not likely to conciliate the party that objected to the ideal tendencies of the theatrical managers. The Jena students, it is true, fresh from the classical dramas, were more than usually loud in applause, and created quite a disturbance in the quiet town. But the critics were all against it, and they were led by the Grand Duke in person. They called it unnatural and tedious, and especially objected to the introduction of the chorus, and the confusion of the religious passages, in which Greek, Christian, and even Mohammedan ideas are found side by side. It is certainly true that in this play Schiller has departed further than in any other of his works from the type of drama naturally expected by the average modern theatregoer. Like many other poets, he was tempted by his admiration of Greek tragedy into an endeavour to reach the grandeur of the original by imitation of its form, forgetting how different are the functions and conditions of the modern stage. Against the charge of being unnatural he considered no defence was needed, since once for all he boldly denied that to hold the mirror up to nature was fit service for art. As to the mixture of religious forms, he pleaded in excuse that in Sicily, the scene of the drama, the pagan traditions lingered long, and much Mohammedanism was introduced, and he adds, in a characteristic passage, that as the substance of all religions always remains the same, the poet has the right of choosing any form that may suit his purpose for the moment. On his use of the chorus he wrote a short essay that was prefixed to the printed editions of the play, and is perhaps the best and simplest statement of his dramatic ideal. Having repeated his main positions that the function of art is to bring before the imagination the essential that is hidden in experience, and, on the other hand, that the stage should make no attempt at reality, being throughout a pleasing deception, as is proved by the employment of rhythm, he goes on to maintain that these apparently contradictory conditions may best be fulfilled by the revival of the chorus, which expounds the hidden principles of justice, and at the same time is the surest defence against naturalism. He even goes so far as to say that the introduction of a chorus would, for the first time, give Shakspeare's tragedies their true significance. He also tries to defend himself for his departure from general classical custom in making his chorus play a personal as well as an ideal part in the tragedy. But Madame de Staël has pointed out the error of this. The two bands of the followers of the hostile brothers do not really represent the "ideal spectator," or the voice of common humanity, as in the Greek chorus, but take a personal and violent share in the main action. Except that they occasionally burst into a lyric ode, they have hardly more title to the name of chorus than the troopers in *Wallenstein*.

In the plot Schiller's object had been, taking the *Œdipus Tyrannus* as his model, to devise a story that could be worked out on the old Greek lines The idea of the "hostile brothers" had been used in many a poem and drama, from the legend of the sons of Œdipus down to Schiller's own *Robbers*, but it suited his purpose well. Don Manuel and Don Cæsar are the two sons of the late Prince of Messina, and from boyhood they have been at deadly variance, for a curse lay on their mother's marriage, and no fruits of it could come to good. The play opens with promise of brighter days, for the bitter feud is at last reconciled by the mother, the widowed Isabella, who is the Jocasta of the play. That her joy may be full, she sends for her daughter Beatrice, who had been kept hidden and unknown in a convent since babyhood, when it was supposed that she had been put to death, because a dream from heaven had foretold the disasters she should bring upon her race. But another prophecy, promising that she should unite the brothers in love, had tempted the mother, blind of heart, to play the old Greek game of trying to trick the oracles while still deeply believing in them. And now a double doom is fulfilled. Unwitting what they did, both brothers have secretly seen and loved their sister. She is already Don Manuel's affianced bride; and, after the glad reconciliation, Don Cæsar, going to claim her for his own, finds her in his brother's arms, and stabs him to the heart. With stately lamentation the half-chorus of his followers bears the body to his mother's feet, checking the current of her joy. Their song, like the choruses in *Samson Agonistes*, is partly unrhymed; and the beginning may be quoted as an example of Schiller's use of the choral ode:

> "Through the streets of the cities,
> Whilst pain follows close,
> Disaster comes striding,
> Or silently lurks
> Round the dwellings of men.
> To-day she is knocking
> At this gate, to-morrow
> Knocking at that,
> And none may escape that is human.
> Sooner or later
> She bringeth her message,
> Unsought for, uncalled,
> To the threshold of each
> That is man born of woman."

Isabella, unconscious of the truth, curses the murderous hand with tragic irony, and pours out against heaven the impious reproaches that are the dramatic justification of her woe. The chorus warns her to be still, but she cries:

> "I will not bridle in my tongue, but loud,
> As my heart bids, give utterance to my thought.
> Why do we tread the houses of the gods,
> And lift to heaven the pious hand of prayer?
> Good, easy fools, what have we won thereby

> For all our faith? It were no harder task
> To speed an arrow to the hornèd moon
> Than touch the hearts of those high-dwelling gods.
> A rampart bars the ken of mortal man,
> And not a prayer may pierce that welkin's brass.
> What profits whether birds fly right or left,
> Or that the stars roll thus or thus their course?
> In nature's book we read but jumbled words :
> The art of dreams is dream, the omens lie."

Horror on horror is slowly brought to light with true tragic power, the audience, conscious of the truth, watching with tragic emotion as the revelation comes home to the unconscious victims. At the end Don Cæsar finds in death by his own hand a refuge from the insupportable hopelessness and shame. The doom of the house is accomplished, the word of heaven upheld, and the vanity of the endeavour to stifle the cruel spawn of error is proved. For beauty of language, for the classic use of irony, and for artistic completeness of form, the *Bride of Messina* has been deservedly ranked as the highest of all Schiller's dramas; and in these points it may well claim to be the first of German tragedies.

Soon after its completion Schiller began to work upon the subject of *Tell*, but during the following winter he was very much interrupted by the presence of Madame de Staël in Weimar. Driven from her own country by the rigour of Napoleon, she came in December 1803—the month of Herder's death—with a fixed determination to discover in Germany the solid intellectual and moral virtues so lacking to France. Like another Tacitus, she would use Germany as an ideal community through which to satirise the vices of her own people. To Weimar she was naturally attracted by the reputation of its poets. Schiller had awaited her arrival with anxiety. In November he wrote to Goethe: "If only she understands German, I do not doubt that we shall get the better of her; but to expound our religion to her in French phrases, and stand our ground against her French volubility, would be too hard a task. We couldn't finish with her so easily as Schelling did with Camille Jourdan, who attacked him armed with Locke. '*Je méprise Locke*,' said Schelling, and his adversary was of course reduced to silence."

But the lady refused to come down from her vantage-ground, and the conversations were conducted in French. In her book on Germany, besides criticisms of his plays, she has left full accounts of her intercourse with Schiller, and her high estimate of his character: how at first she took him for a general on account of his court uniform: how he discussed the French drama with her in slow and demure sentences, quite unabashed by his villainous treatment of the language. During the winter they became very intimate. It was impossible to reject her homage or escape her fascination. Writing again to Goethe, who, for the most part, kept out of the way at Jena, he praises her sincerity and freedom from all affectation.

"In all that we call philosophy one is continually at variance with her, and no amount of argument can reconcile us. But her nature and feeling are better than her metaphysics. She will explain, inspect, and measure everything. She allows of nothing hard or unfathomable; and what she cannot illumine with her torch, for her has no existence. She has therefore a natural horror of the Ideal Philosophy, which, she maintains, leads to mysticism and superstition, and such things choke her like nitrogen.

For what we call poetry she has no sense. . . . The great difficulty is the most extraordinary rapidity of her tonuge: one has to become simply an organ of hearing to follow her."

As time went on, this flood of words wore out his patience. Whilst admitting her to be the most cultured and intellectual of feminine creatures, he began to long pathetically for her departure, and to threaten that she might find fickleness even in Germans; and when at last she went, he felt as though he had recovered from a severe illness.

"On the mountains is freedom"—the cry of the chorus in the *Bride of Messina*—might be taken as the motto of Schiller's last great dramatic poem, *William Tell*, which was finished in February 1804, and acted at Weimar in the following month. The legend of Tell had suggested itself to Goethe as a fit subject for epic during his visit to Switzerland in 1797, but, with his usual magnanimous indifference to personal considerations, he had abandoned his intention of writing on it himself in favour of his friend. Accordingly he gave Schiller every encouragement, especially describing to him the scenery and local customs of the district where the action is laid. For the story itself Schiller went to the main source of the legend in Tscudi's *Chronicon Helveticum*, a naïve and uncritical sixteenth-century history of Switzerland that had been carefully edited and reprinted at Basel in 1734. Here he found nearly all the incidents, and most of the characters, that he introduced into the drama. In some passages the language also is almost identical. He used the chronicle much as Shakspeare used Holinshed, and in certain points we may see that he was equally hampered by his authority to the detriment of his art.

The story of Tell's exploits, to which the innocent Tscudi confidently assigned the date 1307-8, has been satisfactorily proved by scientific historians and comparative mythologists to be merely a variety of an ancient myth, common to other nations, but embellished in Switzerland by the addition of later legends. Schiller's poem has, nevertheless, made it so popular, it remains so familiar to every child, so entirely true to every unsuspicious and humble nature, that it is unnecessary here to recapitulate the incidents of the plot. The treatment throughout is epic rather than dramatic. It abounds in narration, and, like the greater part of *Wallenstein*, might be described as an epic in dialogue. No one would call it a comedy; nor is it a tragedy, for in this alone, of all Schiller's plays, the end is happy, and though the interest culminates in Gessler's death, he is not allowed to excite enough sympathy to make him a truly tragic figure. For the rest, it is noticeable that Schiller has here entirely thrown off the classic traditions that had guided him in the *Bride of Messina*. The chorus has disappeared; and, instead of inexorable fate, we find, as motive for the whole, the miraculous power of the individual will, and the stir of a brave and honest people rising in successful resistance to intolerable wrongs. The chilling and oppressive idea of an unyielding destiny, against which the noblest efforts of mortal man fall impotent, is removed, and the whole poem is pervaded by a cheerful hopefulness, a confidence in the ultimate power of good, and in the strength as well as the beauty of virtue, that had not been so prominent in Schiller's works since the days of *Don Carlos*.

But there is now no note of vague cosmopolitan

enthusiasm and universal brotherhood, as in *Don Carlos*, still less of wild rebellion against mankind, and youthful hopes of some impalpable millennium beyond the chaos of blood, as in the *Robbers*. Here all is definite, solid, and attainable. The Teuton has taken the place of the Celt. Much of the charm has gone, and with it nearly all the rhetoric and magnificence of phrase. At a drawing-room meeting of anarchists in the suburbs, none of the patriot rebels in *Tell* would cut such a figure as Karl Moor or the Marquis of Posa. Their aims are not abstract nor particularly ideal. They are entirely unselfconscious; even their patriotism and nationality are hardly formulated into principles. The rights for which they strive are not the Rights of Man, but the historic privileges of their fathers. Their watchword is not Liberty, but Freedom, not Equality and Fraternity, but wife and child and home. The wrongs that goad them on are not the theoretic imaginations of economists or men of letters, but the stolen oxen, the threatened house, the blinded father, the rising fortress, the violated chamber, the son set up as a father's mark. In these Swiss heroes we have a race of simple mountain peasants, idealised, it is true, but not past recognition. There is very little of pastoral sentimentality about them, still less of French revolutionary tirade. Schiller has absorbed the spirit of the old chronicle so entirely that he rises above the magnificent weaknesses generally characteristic of himself and his age. And, again, he has so entirely absorbed Goethe's descriptions of Swiss scenery that the background of the poem is no less truthful. In the very first scene we are placed in the midst of a land of mountains, and lakes, and flowering meadows. The cows are coming down from the Alp, proud of their tinkling bells. The sound of the Ranz-des-vaches is in the air. A storm is sweeping up through the gates of the hills, and above stand the silver horns where "death and morning" walk. Fisher-boy and cowherd and hunter pass onto the stage with little bursts of song that are amongst the loveliest lyrics that Schiller ever wrote.*

To a German audience also the use of the Swiss words and, to some extent, of the Swiss dialect, with its tender diminutives and curtailed endings, would bring a vision of wooden chalets huddled round bulbous spires shining with metal plates. All through the play we are not allowed to forget the scene and its influence on the heart of the people. And yet the descriptive passages are brief and scarce. With singular self-restraint, Schiller has almost entirely refrained from eloquent passages on the grandeur and sublimity of mountain scenery. To his peasants, as to all primitive and healthy people who scrape their living from the patient earth, the dangerous

---

* We may notice the parallel and difference between the first verse of the fisher's song,

"Da hört er ein Klingen,
Wie Flöten so süss,
Wie Stimmen der Engel
Im Paradies,"

and the familiar lines in the *Ancient Mariner* (1797)—

"And now 'twas like all instruments,
Now like a lonely flute,
And now it is an angel's song,
That makes the heavens be mute."

and barren tracts of rock and snow are mainly objects of terror or disgust. For them true beauty, like love, is of the valley, and lies in the strips of fertile plain, or kindly slope above the torrent's reach.

Just as the tempest has begun to blot out the sunshine and lash the lake in the opening scene, a man rushes in and entreats to be ferried across. He has slain one of the foreign tyrants for an insult to his wife. The pursuers are close upon him; delay is death; yet none dare launch on such a water. Then Tell enters, and without waste of words he does what all would wish to do, and no one had done. The action is characteristic of the man. In Tell, Schiller produced his noblest creation, different as the type is from all his earlier ideals of greatness. Like the Tell of the chronicle, who was called Tell because he had but little wit, he is a man of few words, of deep, unspoken thoughts, but few ideas. Averse to schemes and plots, he takes no part in the patriotic conspiracy; but when the moment for deeds comes, he is ready. Bred up from childhood within arms-reach of death, he has the simplicity and seriousness of an old sailor. He never doubts, nor hesitates, nor argues the other side of the question. As confident of the right as Ivan Ivanovitch, in Mr. Browning's poem, he acts without reasons and without excuses, because he can do no other. He is calm and unperplexed, as one who is guided by the voice of God. The well-known scene at the end of the fourth act, where he sits waiting with his trusty bow for Gessler to pass along the Hollow Way, is unsurpassed for simple grandeur and tragic power in all Schiller's work.

> "Here, through this hollow lane, he needs must pass.
> There is no other road to Küssnacht. Here
> I'll make an end. The place well fits the need."

Deep thoughts of his past life, of his wife and children, of the cruel wrongs that are driving him to kill a man instead of the mountain game, flow through his mind. He watches how others pass in unconscious ignorance up and down the road.

> "Here on this bench of stone I sit me down—
> A moment's haven on the wanderer's way—
> For here there's no abiding—man by man,
> Each passes each with quick unfriending tread,
> Nor asks him of his grief. By this road comes
> The merchant's heavy care, and pilgrim poor,
> Whose scrip's his all; by this, the pious monk,
> The thief, night's comrade, and the fiddler gay,
> The packman with his heavy-laden beast,
> Wending from unknown lands of distant men,
> For every path leads to the world's confine;
> They go their way, and each man followeth
> His business such as it is—and mine is death."

A sound of merry music is heard, for a wedding is coming that way. A gossip stops and chatters to him as he waits. A poor woman with her starving brood takes up her station, waiting also for the tyrant, but with supplications for pity. Her husband is "a poor wild hayman of the Rigiberg," who, swinging his scythe over the precipice, harvests the unclaimed grass—a trade more dreadful than his who gathered samphire on the Dover cliffs—and now for months he has lain in the dungeon untried and innocent. Gessler comes, and she throws herself in his way, but her entreaties are vain. Uttering curses and threats against this rebellious people, he is about to ride over her, when Tell's arrow finds its home in his heart. The marriage music continues for a time, and then suddenly stops. Monks enter and bear off the body, chanting the dirge of death that makes all humanity one.

It would have been better to have brought the drama to an end here. After such a scene, the fifth act, even when it describes the triumph of a liberated people, is necessarily an anti-climax. And, unfortunately, Schiller, in order to mark the difference between his patriot and the ordinary selfish assassin, has introduced the episode of John of Austria seeking refuge in Tell's house after the murder of his uncle the Emperor. The contrast is not needed, for Tell himself is his own sufficient justification. Again, there is the further episode of the union of Bertha and Rudenz in mutual affection and devotion to their people's good. Complying with the modern notion that no great action can be of interest without an admixture of the love between man and woman, Schiller has throughout woven a thin under-plot from the story of their courtship. But it introduces a false note quite out of harmony with the rest of the poem, and from first to last it may be omitted with advantage.

In April 1804, a week or two after *Tell* had been acted, Schiller set off for Berlin with his wife and two boys. In Berlin his dramas had of late years attained their greatest success. Tired of the pettiness of Weimar and its little round of gossip, he was much attracted by the stir and fulness and large interests of a great capital city, where the stimulus to production would be keener, and it would be possible to escape observation. The welcome he received encouraged him to hope for a permanent position there. A performance of the *Bride of Messina* in his presence was made the occasion for an ovation even more enthusiastic than at Leipzig. All society, from the King and Queen downwards, received him with honour; his boys played with the little princes, who were afterwards to become Frederick William IV. and the Emperor William. But his wife, remembering the shores of Vevey and the pleasant hills beside the Saale, was oppressed by the dreary city and the sandy plain, and could find no beauty in the great reaches of wandering river, the wide heaths, and long forests of monotonous pine. As they drove home, she burst into tears at the sight of the first hill-top rising blue above the level. Schiller himself, too, on his return, found that at his age a man should not hastily tear himself up by the roots, and that the bonds of old friendships are not readily broken. As often happens, signs of appreciation, unexpressed or unnoticed before, came home to him after his absence. Goethe urged him to stay; the Grand-Duke largely increased his income. At last he wrote to Berlin offering to go there only for a few months every year, and that for a high salary. As he probably expected, no notice was taken of his letter, and he determined to remain in Weimar "for the rest of his life." He had still about eleven months to live.

CHAPTER VIII.

SOME few weeks after their return from Berlin, the Schillers visited their old home in Jena. Here, in July, their second daughter was born; but at her birth her father was already a dying man. A short time before he had driven down the vale of the Saale as far as the castle-crowned cliffs of Dornburg, in the hot afternoon of a German midsummer; and as he returned in the evening, he was struck by the same fatal influence that created in that valley the tradition of the "Erlking." For he was touched by the cold white mist—the "Nebelstreif" of Goethe's ballad—that hangs in wreaths over the flat, damp meadows along the riverside. The attack was merely a violent return of the feverish chill to which he had long been subject, and after a few days of intense agony he appeared to be regaining his strength as usual. But his sister-in-law observed that after this his face turned a leaden grey; and, in fact, he never recovered. Through the winter his power of work gradually failed him; his blood seemed to be curdled and torpid, and he could only beguile the weary time with the translation of *Phèdre*. In November, however, he roused himself, at Goethe's entreaty, to compose a little masque, called the *Homage of the Arts*, as a welcome to Weimar's future Duchess, the Princess Marie of Russia, daughter of the Czar Paul, who had been murdered in 1801.

Sometimes, too, on easier days, released for a while from pain or numbness, he would return with vigour to the serious drama into which he had plunged with his usual impetuosity immediately after the completion of *Tell*. It was to be called *Demetrius*, or *Dmitri*, and its plot was suggested by the general interest in things Russian at Weimar during the Hereditary Grand-Duke's courtship.

Like the drama of *Perkin Warbeck*, which Schiller had long intended to write, the tragedy of *Demetrius* is the story of a pretender's failure. The False Dmitri of Russian history gave himself out to be the only surviving son of Ivan the Terrible, and under this title claimed the throne at the beginning of the seventeenth century. Trusting to the support of Poland, and a pretended recognition by his reputed mother, he made war on the Czar Boris, who had been minister to Ivan's eldest son, Feodor, and had almost certainly put the true Dmitri to death for his own advantage. During the war Boris died from some unknown cause, and Dmitri appeared to have attained the height of his ambition, till his imposture was suspected, and he was killed in the rising that ultimately led to the accession of the Romanow dynasty. Schiller, in his sketch of the drama, has followed history without much deviation, and it has supplied him with perhaps the finest dramatic material that he ever treated. Had the tragedy been finished, the interest would have centred in the development of the character of Demetrius, who, in the first act, is introduced laying his claims before the Polish Assembly in all the bright confidence of honesty and conscious right. Inspired by his integrity, and their ancient hatred for the Muscovite, the Poles adopt his cause with chivalrous impetuosity, though only after a scene of disorderly excitement and turmoil, such as in Schiller's own day had caused the name of Poland to be obliterated from the roll of nations. Part of the cause of Demetrius' ultimate failure was his mistake in employing an army of unstable Poles against his own impassive but unyielding countrymen. But the root of the tragedy was hidden in his own heart. He had entered Russia full of the high hope and noble purposes of one of Schiller's typical heroes. He freely devotes his future to the cause of peace and the happiness of his subjects. He hears with tender commiseration of his rival's overthrow and suicide. But just when the final triumph seems secure, and he is about to enter the sphere of empire as befits a philosophic and patriot king, he learns the true story of his birth, and of the craft that had substituted him in early boyhood for the murdered prince. The one agent of the deed, in expectation of reward, himself reveals the secret of the fraud, and for reward Demetrius strikes him dead. Supposing that the truth died with him, the Czar, a mock Czar now, in an evil moment, determines to play out the part; but in his own heart and brain the truth still lives, and will not suffer itself to be forgotten. Thence in the outline of the plot we can trace a noble nature's rapid corruption, spreading from the one speck of conscious deceit till each single virtue has been infected in turn.

Confidence, bravery, and kindness forsake him. Distrust in himself breeds the distrust of others, and he is on the way to become a common faithless and brutal tyrant, when fortunately the rising discontent gathers head in the conspiracy that ends the misery of his deception by the surest way.

It is evident that such a character belongs to an altogether different class from the tragic heroes of Schiller's other dramas. There is far more complexity in it, far more scope for analysis. It is a theme worthy of Mr. Browning, and, if Schiller had lived to elaborate the conception, it would have been interesting to contrast his treatment of the subject with *A Soul's Tragedy* or *The Return of the Druses*. The deceit of Demetrius would not have been so entirely selfish as Chiappino's, nor have come so near true patriotism as Djabal's. Both he and Djabal are saved by death, if by death alone, from the completeness of Chippiano's ruin. On the other hand, though not such a noble figure as the wily but impassioned Druse, he is perhaps more truly pitiable, for he falls from perfect innocence to lower corruption; whereas Djabal is conscious of his imposture throughout, and yet never quite gives up belief in himself. We cannot, of course, expect from Schiller the unerring subtlety and refinement of Mr. Browning's mental analysis. His gifts were of an entirely different order. Nevertheless, it is possible that, had the play been finished, the character of Demetrius would have been accounted the subtlest, though not the most attractive, creation of Schiller's dramatic power.

Nor is the outline of Demetrius himself the only sign

in this fragment that the poet's insight into the reality and variety of life was now at its strongest, and was likely to have increased in depth year by year. We may wonder what form would ultimately have been taken by Marina, the cruel Polish girl, with dark far-reaching designs, one of the very few evil-minded women in Schiller's works. Endowed with insatiable lust of power, with a loveless jealousy more cruel than the grave, with a supreme command over the hearts and wills of men, she was to have crept to her place on the throne at Demetrius's side through strategem, treachery, and blood; and once mounted there, was to have told him that she had known him all along to be an impostor—had known it even whilst he was himself honest in his ignorance. And then, again, what depth of pathos might have been reached in Marfa, the widowed and childless queen, to whom, in her ice-bound convent, the news is brought with the first breath of spring that her little son, her murdered Dmitri, is not dead, but is now on his way with armies, that hail him as their Czar, to release her from the monotonous winter of a life whose hopes and fears belong only to the past. Incredulous, but desperate with longing, she forces herself to believe what she knows cannot be true. Then, with wild joy, she bursts out into the soliloquy that was perhaps the last verse Schiller ever wrote, for the sheet, written in his usual beautifully legible character, and carefully corrected, was found, after his death, lying open upon his desk—

> "He comes, he comes, and armies on him wait,
> To bring me freedom, and avenge my shame!
> List to his drum, his trumpet's stern alarm!
> O list, ye peoples, to a monarch's call!

> Come from the orient and the noonday sun,
> Come from your steppes and everlasting forests,
> Of every tongue, of every various garb!
> Bridle the horse, the reindeer, and the camel!
> Come like the innumerable ocean waves,
> And gather to the standard of your king,
> Like snowflakes fluttering 'neath the wintry star.
>
> O, wherefore stand I here in fetters bound,
> Helpless, whilst endless passion stirs my soul?
> O sun immortal, round this earthly globe
> Driving thy daily course, bear thou my words!
> O breeze, that blowest where thou listest, free,
> An instant messenger to furthest goal,
> O bear my warmth of longing to his heart!
> Nought have I but my prayer and my complaint,
> Springing like flame from out my bosom's depth,
> With trust in God I turn them unto heaven.
> A mother's tears, tears and a mother's blessing
> Are all my portion here, and like armed men
> I send them out to bring him on his way."

Her joy and confidence are short-lived. When she meets Demetrius, he has already learnt the truth about his birth, and some indefinable instinct tells her that he is consciously acting a lie. Still, in spite of misery and hesitation, she cannot altogether abandon the new-born hope, but forces herself to share in the pretender's triumph. From the point of view of stage requirements, the part throughout would have afforded the finest opportunities for a great actress. The climax would have been reached when Romanow's conspirators burst into her presence, whilst Demetrius is by her side, and demand of her, on the sacred emblems, whether he is in truth her son. Not feeling for Demetrius the love of Anael for the Druse, she is incapable of her splendid lie. She remains silent, and the next moment he falls pierced with swords at her feet.

For Schiller that winter of 1804-5 passed slowly and heavily away; but, as he wrote to Körner, when the ice began to thaw, his heart and thoughts seemed to thaw too. The Spring, the inexhaustible theme of the old German poets, does not come in central Germany tentatively as with us, here advancing and there drawing back like the tide on the shore, but with a sudden blaze of verdure and burst of song. To Schiller also it brought new life. He longed to see the sea and Switzerland before he died. As soon as he was able to go out, he went to visit Goethe, who, like himself, had come very near to death during the last few months. When they met they said nothing about their health, but only discussed plans for the future. On April the 29th Goethe returned the visit, and found Schiller just starting for the theatre. Not strong enough to sit through the performance himself, Goethe accompanied him to the door, and there they parted forever. That night Schiller was attacked by another feverish chill, and on May-day it became evident that the case was even more serious than usual. He still continued to work, writing verses for *Demetrius*, or listening whilst his wife or sister-in-law read to him; but from day to day his strength visibly declined. On the eighth, when asked how he felt, he replied, evidently referring to his mental state, " Better and better, more and more cheerful," and in the evening he told them to draw the curtain that he might see the light of sunset. Except some terms of endearment to his wife, those were perhaps his last conscious words; his last petition, like Goethe's, was for light. Next day he was wandering in mind, and spoke mostly in Latin. Towards six o'clock in the afternoon he died. "Death," he had said with characteristic optimism, "can be no evil, for it is universal."

The tidings were at once taken to Goethe's house, but no one dared to tell him of the truth. Seeing from the looks of his household that something was wrong, he said at once, "Schiller is worse." There was no answer, and he said again, "I see that Schiller must be very ill." The remainder of the evening he spent in silence, and that night he was heard weeping in his room. Next morning he said, "He is dead, then." Three weeks later, in writing to Zelter, he said, referring to his own recent illness, "I thought to have lost myself, and now I have lost a friend, and in him the half of my being." All the interests of his life seemed to have ceased together. One gloomy day succeeded another, and the blank pages of his diary were the most eloquent chronicle of the dreariness of his soul. For a time he tried to cheat himself by an attempt to complete the tragedy of *Demetrius* on the lines that Schiller had laid down. But he was obliged to give it up, and the failure of the effort only increased the heaviness of his grief. "After losses," he once said, "I have tried to go on with my usual work as though nothing had happened, but have always found that in the end one has to pay the debt in full." In August he composed the beautiful tribute to Schiller's memory that served as an *Epilogue* to the *Song of the Bell* after its recitation in the Weimar theatre.* It

---

* It was altered and added to in 1815.

is known to all for the two great lines in which more fitly than in any other possible words the secret of Schiller's power as a man and a poet is set forth :

" Behind him, like an empty show, remained
The Commonplace that holds us all enchained."

From the more obvious forms of the commonplace and vulgar in private life Schiller was saved by a temperament naturally aristocratic and reserved. " Though he has had the fortune to pass for a special friend of the people," said Goethe to Eckermann, " he was in reality far more of an aristocrat than I." Nor will the apparent contradiction surprise us who have known so many true champions of the people who have preferred to carry on the contest at a comfortable distance from their clients. The actual meanness, squalor, and absurdity of the crowd profane would have been to Schiller merely oppressive and abhorrent. There was in him, at all events after he attained maturity, a refined sense of proportion and restraint that made him shudder at the approach of all that might seem common or unclean ; nor had nature endowed him in compensation, as she has sometimes endowed others no less sensitive, with the rich gift of an observant and pitying humour. For him the outer world of every day was neither so elevated nor so interesting as the world of ideas in which he habitually lived surrounded by the theories of philosophers and the high conceptions of his own mind. He was liable to become estranged from the familiar face of nature and the common intercourse of actual men. We read that, plunged in meditation, he would go on his way without the smallest observation or enjoyment of the surrounding scene ; and Goethe tells us that, if expecting a stranger, Schiller would often make himself ill with apprehension, and that when the visitor appeared, he would sometimes become very impatient and even rude. It was the scholar's penalty, the price he paid for the elevation and tension of a mind occupied habitually with interests remote from the common world. Debarred by his own choice, as well as by the conventions of civilisation, from some of the widest sympathies of ordinary men, and from the purifying influences of manual labour, he never attained to the open fearlessness and calm of an entirely healthy and active nature.

Without prying too curiously into the close relations of body and mind, we may say that it is no surprise to us to find traces of the same kind of weakness in the details that have come down to us concerning Schiller's daily life. We detect in them a tone of unhealthiness and strain. The well-worn story that he drew inspiration for his dramas from copious draughts of champagne must be abandoned in the face of his sister-in-law's definite statement that he never touched wine while writing ; but she admits that at his desk he generally drank coffee, which was probably at least equally pernicious. Too often he worked far into the night, in feverish excitement, instead of awaiting, like Goethe, the cool hours of morning. In his study at daytime he used to obscure the sunlight by red curtains, the warm glow of which acted, as he imagined, as a stimulant to his creative power. And this morbid craving for artificial excitement sometimes carried him away into further

SCHILLER. 189

absurdities best illustrated by the well-known story in the *Conversations with Eckermann*, where Goethe remarks how differently constituted he was from Schiller in body as well as in mind. "Air that was wholesome to him," he goes on, "was so much poison to me;" and he narrates how once he sat down in Schiller's room to wait for his return, and gradually became so indisposed that he almost fainted. He discovered that a dreadful smell was coming from a cupboard near at hand, and on opening it found that it was full of rotten apples. Schiller's wife coming in soon afterwards, told him that her husband thought the smell beneficial; in fact, that he could neither work nor live without it.

But in spite of his bodily weakness and a few accompanying pecularities of mind and manner, it would be the greatest possible mistake to think of Schiller as a melancholy invalid. When all is said, it remains true that, unlike most of his famous contemporaries, he showed hardly any trace either of hypochondria or insanity. Though his mind never attained the grandeur of Goethe's, nor the keen temper of Lessing's, he was, in all essential points, as sane as either; and though he had no touch of Jean Paul's extravagant humour, nor of his loving pity for things of low estate, he was at bottom as simple and warm-hearted. After his marriage, his family life presents a picture of unselfishness and peace too rare in the biographies of men of letters. His love for wife and children, as well as for the inmates of the old Suabian home, was entirely honest and unaffected. As soon as the frothy paradoxes of youth were laid aside, he took things very simply, and recognised the wholesomeness of natural obligations. In spite of his shy and retiring habits, he would shake off every trace of self-consciousness or moroseness if the social circle in which he found himself were suited to his mind. "He was as great at the tea-table," said Goethe, "as he would have been in the council-chamber. Nothing embarrassed nor constrained him, nor checked the flight of his thoughts. Whatever grand idea he had always flowed out freely, without reserve or hesitation." Above all, in compensation for ill-health, nervousness, and poverty, nature had given him, as he often used to say, an inexhaustible fund of cheerfulness and hope. He had the power of throwing off difficulties, and leaving disappointment behind him. Before the critics had time to say their worst of one work, he was borne far beyond their reach by enthusiasm over the creation of the next; for, like the Athenians of old, he accounted what was accomplished as nothing compared with what was yet to be done.

It was this "inexhaustible cheerfulness," this blessing of a sanguine and yet not impatient temperament, that more truly even than his intellectual ability was the secret of his success. It was this that upheld him in the midst of trials under which men of far higher natural powers have often fallen. It was this that enabled him to withstand the innumerable cares and temptations that beset the path of the man of letters. The irregularity of his work neither drove him to dissipation nor reduced him to impotence. Even in his rare intervals of enforced and tedious leisure he did not allow himself to despair altogether of his art. Even under the stress of writing for money he could forget to be mercenary, and remain an artist. Undaunted by the indifference of the ordinary world and the small apparent effect of things poetical, he retained his high belief in the ultimate value of beauty in thought and word. He owed all, it is true, to a strength of will disciplined from early youth in arms and the school of adversity. He was determined to be a poet, and the same determination that would not let him rest till he had brought a work to conclusion, enabled him to attain to the rank in poetry that is his. But in this strength of will, courageous hope and cheerfulness were the most important elements. From time to time, for short intervals, under the stress of outward circumstance, his purpose seemed to fail him; he forgot the unity of life, and was tempted into by-ways or general diffuseness. It may be questioned whether he could have clung to his object, as some have done, through prolonged years of uninterrupted gloom, of torturing doubt, and hope indefinitely deferred. But above all such things some fortunate gift of temperament had lifted him, in Wilhelm Meister's words, "like a god." Inspired by hope and an unquestioning confidence in the objects of his enthusiasm, in their sufficiency and ultimate triumph, he passed unscathed amidst the perils of indolence, hesitation, and despair, as well as through the ordinary trials of poverty, sickness, and failure. He seemed to bear a charmed life, and the enchantment passed from him to others. Eager and unresting in the pursuit of his ideals, "a new and more complete man every week," he seemed to diffuse energy and enthusiasm as he went, and his presence was to his few associates as inspiring as his works to the rest of his generation. Referring to their friendly intercourse in Weimar and Jena, Goethe once described their manner of existence in those years as "idyllic," by which, perhaps, he meant that life in those quiet little country towns was not only pervaded by a tranquil simplicity and old-world peace under the sweet influences of the natural seasons, but was also transfused by an entirely unselfish passion for beauty and pure knowledge, and all that might be supposed to tend to the fabled perfection of a golden age. "With us," as he wrote to Carlyle in 1829, "it was then a time of unlimited endeavour: no one thought of demanding a reward; our one effort was to do good service."* We need not doubt that to this effort Schiller's influence supplied the main impulse; and when we remember this, when we remember the simplicity and innocence of his life, his single-hearted devotion to knowledge and art, his indifference to all the vulgar tests and evidences of success, such weaknesses and limitations as he had, seem to vanish, and the image of him that remains in our minds is of the earnest, cheerful, and impetuous man, the inspiring friend of Goethe.

If we turn from the man to the writer, the modern Englishman is met, at the outset, by almost insuperable difficulties in an attempt to estimate the true value of Schiller's work. It is perhaps hardly possible, in these days, to appreciate him as highly as his reputation appears to demand. He is still commonly used, it is true, as a text-book for schools, because he wrote good German, and has received from Propriety her meed

* Cf. Prof. MaxMüller's *Opening Address to the English Goethe Society*. *Contemporary Review*, June 1886.

of honour, that "there is no harm in him." But serious students would probably admit that few poets of equal fame are now less studied for their own sake. His name remains familiar to all, because it has been consecrated by its connection with a genius higher than his own—a genius more closely in sympathy with the thought of recent years. But otherwise the present age is generally content to remain ignorant of him, and could hardly understand where the secret of his reputed greatness lay. For the present age has been called essentially unimaginative, while it was to imagination only that Schiller made his appeal. The present age justly plumes itself on its realism; while against realism Schiller declared it was his special mission to do battle. The scientific spirit has entered into literature, and before all else we demand clearness, accuracy, and exact analysis; while Schiller is sometimes obscure, often inaccurate, and never analytic. Guided by our own experience of modern life, we are constrained to circumscribe the heroic within very close limits, and like *genre* painters contemplating the vast conceptions of old-fashioned allegoric art, we regard the ideal forms of Schiller's drama with melancholy or indifference. The high emotions, the hopes and passions which he stirred in the hearts of our grandfathers, seem in us to be dead of atrophy. It is difficult, if not impossible, to put ourselves back to the time when Carlyle, in his beautiful and enthusiastic *Life of Schiller*, gave to the world the firstfruits and earnest of his greatness. Our hopes from German literature are no longer so high as in the days when Goethe was still alive, and the words of his fellows were welcomed by many as revelations of a new gospel of art and wisdom. Their work has now for a long time past been either absorbed or rejected. It is true that German thought has as much influence, and in the near future is likely to have more, than at any previous time. Now, however, it no longer works through literature, but through science, arms, and social ideas. In literature for the last thirty years we have been gradually but steadily returning to the French alliance, so that, for the younger generation, it must require a distinct effort of historical imagination to realise the awe and reverence with which their elders used to approach the German poets and essayists as though they hoped to find in them the secret oracles of the unknown. If members of the younger generation venture at all into these regions, they know very well that—if we may again borrow an illustration from Wilhelm Meister—they only go to seek their fathers' asses; though it is still possible that, as by accident, they may find a kingdom in the search.

How far it may also be true that Germany is beginning to forget Schiller, as Matthew Arnold accused us of forgetting Byron, we will not venture to say. There are, at all events, but few external signs of it as yet. The German mind, still retaining a love of the ideal, finds in Schiller's heroic creations a satisfaction unknown to more realistic peoples; and German literature, with all its high merits, has been throughout so deficient in dramatic power, so obscure in the outline of character, compared with other European literatures, that the importance of such dramatic production as it possesses is likely to become a little exaggerated in popular opinion. And yet it may perhaps be said of Schiller, as of Byron, that his most striking and obvious service was for his own time rather than for the future; and here perhaps we may discover the truth lying at the bottom of those words of Goethe that otherwise may appear strange to us now : "There is no writer in any literature to whom Schiller can be exactly compared, but he comes nearest to Byron." At first sight few poets would seem to have less in common. Yet they were alike in this—that both gave an impulse of freedom and energy to the thought and literature of their time. Both regarded themselves as champions of liberty; both were engaged in the same revolt, though armed with different weapons; both inspired youth with a strange enthusiasm, though the sources of inspiration in both were not the same. Schiller, it is true, long outlived his early passion of revolt; in him hope took the place of disgust, and cynicism had no part in his nature. But he did not make peace with the powers of the world, nor become a mere spectator in the struggle, though, as is natural to poets, he may have exaggerated the power of words, and thought that the strife was over as soon as the battle-cry was chosen, and the word of command given. There was, therefore, for his contemporaries something inspired and prophetic in his works, and they heard in all his dramas the same high tone of courage. We may hear it still, in *Tell* as in *The Robbers ;* but for us it has not the same significance. To us it is like the sound of " battles long ago," for other forces have come to the front, and the struggle has changed its place and method, though not its purpose.

But Schiller was not only a destroyer and liberator;

he fulfilled yet another and more distinctive function of Apollo. He was a purifier; and it was by his work of purification that his influence became most permanent. It was this that made him a classic, and gave him a share in moulding the language and thought of a great people. The purifiers of literature are, it is true, seldom popular; they have "no cunning art to stir the blood;" they seldom approach the themes that take the crowd, the common sources of tears and laughter. Sometimes, as in the case of Milton and Schiller himself, their high reputation amongst generations of poets and critics has imposed, as it were, a canon of belief in them upon the mass of the people, so that to be ignorant of them is to be thought uneducated; but many who openly acknowledge them are at heart reluctant, and secretly think them monotonous, cold, and dull. Yet their service may none the less be of the highest; for in literature excellence cannot be tested by the counting of heads. And Schiller acted upon the literature of Germany as a purifier both in thought and word. Though his verse is, as a rule, too facile for perfection, though only a few of his lyrics reach the highest melody of which the language became capable in the hands of Goethe or Heine, though his dramatic line sometimes loses in dignity for want of compression, he did as much as any other to save the language from the curious quaintness so tempting to German writers, whilst his very weakness, such as it was, prevented him from falling into the petty adornments and elaborate prettinesses that characterise so much of modern literature. And so also in his choice of subject, whether for lyric or drama, he was not the slave of details nor of futile subtleties, but was continually occupied with great central ideas. These of themselves gave to his work a breadth and grandeur of tone, all the more needed in modern times, when, as he complained in the introduction to the *Bride of Messina*, people live in private, and the gods have withdrawn into the heart. It was his endeavour to raise art and poetry from their shameful service as handmaids to private comfort, and restore them to their stern and high functions in public life. His success was only partial, for the tide of modern life was set against him; but the effort has gained its reward. For, unlike Wordsworth as Schiller was in nearly every point, a German may almost say of him, as Professor Seeley has said of Wordsworth, that no modern writer has done more to redeem our life from vulgarity.*

* *Natural Religion*, p. 103.

INDEX.

A.

Abraham à Santa Clara, 134

B.

Ballads, 120-126
Bell, Song of the, 152-154, 164
Berlin, 177, 178
Bride of Messina, produced, 165; critical objections, 166; plot, 167-169; contrast to *Tell*, 172; performance at Berlin, 178
Byron, 194, 195

C.

Carlyle, on German drama, 55; contrast with Schiller, 59; on German metaphysics, 94; *Life of Schiller*, 195
Coleridge, 33, 121, 174

D.

Demetrius, historical source, 180; character of Demetrius, 181, 182; Marina and Marfa, 183, 184
Don Carlos, completed, 50; incongruities, 53, 54; plot, 54; the Marquis of Posa, 55-57; Philip, 57, 58; contrast with *Tell*, 173

F.

Fichte, 75, 91, 106
Fiesco, production of, 26; character and plot, 36-38

G.

Ghost-seer, 63
Gleim, 106
Goethe, effect of his early works on Schiller, 19; visits the

Military Academy, 20; *Werther*, 26, 27; despair at success of the *Robbers*, 35, 100; in Italy, 61; secures Schiller's appointment at Jena, 72; indifference to Schiller at first, 98; dislike of his early works, 100; promises assistance in *The Hours*, 101; conversation on the "symbolic plant," 101, 102; rapid growth of friendship, 103-105; contributions to *The Hours*, 107; partnership in the *Xenia*, 109-114; on Schiller's house at Jena, 119; management of Weimar theatre, 163; Kotzebue, 164; assistance in *Tell*, 171; last meeting with Schiller, 185; effect of news of Schiller's death, 186; attempt to continue *Demetrius*, 186

H.

Hegel, 75
Heine, 121, 196
Herder, 26, 61, 106, 113, 115, 116, 169
Hours, The, 90, 91, 96, 101, 105, 107, 115
Humboldt, 75, 105, 149

J.

Jacobi, 106
Jena, Schiller's appointment as Professor, 73; situation, 74; University, 75; unhealthy for Schiller, 84; his last visit, 179

K.

Kalb, Frau von, 45, 61, 77
Kant, Schiller's opposition to his ethics, 52, 89; service to philosophy, 53; his exponent Reinhold, 61; influence at Jena, 75, 87; effect on Schiller, 87, 88; *Critique of the Power of Judgment*, 89; commentators, 112
Knights of Malta, 127
Körner, first intercourse with Schiller, 46; friendship at Dresden, 49; character, 49, 50; parting with Schiller, 60; danger of rupture, 77; visited by Schiller, 86; correspondence on æsthetics, 90; Schiller's last visit, 162; letter in 1805, 185
Kotzebue, 164

L.

Lavater, 108, 112
Lengefeld, 64-70
Lessing, 11, 19, 43, 90, 111, 112, 113, 163, 189
Ludwigsburg, Court at, 13, 14, 96

INDEX. 201

M.

Macbeth, 150, 151
Maid of Orleans, plot contrasted with history, 159, 160; subordinate characters, 161; performance at Leipzig, 162
Maria Stuart, studies for, 151; translation of, 154; reception, 157; plot, 158
Mellish, 154
Milton, 154, 196
Moniteur, 44
Muses' Almanack, 110, 115, 120, 152

N.

Napoleon, 145, 155
Nicolai, 108, 111

P.

Perkin Warbeck, 180
Phèdre, 163, 179
Plot and Passion, production of, 26; the plot, 38-40; compared to Miss Sara Samson, 43
Plutarch, 19, 29, 67
Prussia, King and Queen of, 151, 178

R.

Reinwald, 25
Resignation, 51
Revolt of the Netherlands, 63, 82

Richter, Jean Paul, 66, 139, 189
Robbers, The, first scenes of, 19; completed, 22; acted at Mannheim, 22; general tendency, 26, 27; plot, 28, 34; Karl Moor, 29, 30; Franz Moor, 28, 33; extraordinary success and influence, 35, 36; contrast with Tell, 173
Roche, Sophie de la, 70
Rousseau, 11, 19, 34, 36, 48, 60, 61, 65, 67
Rudolstadt, 62, 64, 65, 66, 74

S.

Schelling, 75, 170
Schiller, Charlotte, Schiller's wife; their first meeting, 62, 64; her sister Karoline, 64; portrait, 65; pursuits, 67
Schiller, Friedrich, birth and parentage, 11, 12; father in the Duke of Würtemberg's service, 12, 13; the court at Ludwigsburg, 13, 14; first attempts at rhyme, 15; the Military Academy, 16, 19; effect of military training, 18, 19; study of medicine, 17; passion for literature, 19; youthful gloom, 20; army surgeon, 20; personal appearance, 20; the Anthology and completion of The Robbers, 22; it is acted at Mannheim,

22; flight from Stuttgart, 23; extreme poverty, 24; refuge at Bauerbach, 25; return to Mannheim, 25; *Fiesco* and *Plot and Passion*, 26; influence of "Storm and Stress" in early works, 26, 27, 43; the three early plays, 27, 40; early lyrics, 40, 42; the diploma of citizenship, 44; the *Thalia*, 45; departure from Mannheim, 46; friendship with Körner, 46, 50; at Leipzig and Dresden, 48, 49; *Hymn to Joy*, 47; *Don Carlos*, 50; *Philosophic Letters*, 52; hopes of humanity, 58-60; first residence in Weimar, 60; meeting with his future wife, 62; study of history, 62; *Revolt of the Netherlands*, 63; *Ghost-seer*, 63; friendship with the Lengefeld family, 64; residence at Volkstädt and Rudolstadt, 69; study of Greek literature, 69; *The Celebrated Woman*, 70; *The Gods of Greece* and *The Artists*, 71; Professorship of History at Jena, 73; first Lecture, 76; diminution in class, 77; betrothal, 78; marriage, 78; historical works, 80-83; beginning of illness, 84; translations from the *Æneid*, 85; gift from Denmark, 85, 86; study of Kant, 87; æsthetic essays, 90-93; effect of the study of philosophy, 93-95; visit to Suabia, 95, 96; previous antipathy to Goethe, 98, 99; beginning of intercourse, 101-105; editor of *The Hours*, 105-107; the *Xenia*, 109-114; new lyrics, 114-116; father's death, 118, 119; new house, 119; ballads, 120-125; lyrics, 126; composition of *Wallenstein*, 127; typical characters, 141, 142; adaptation of *Macbeth*, 151; *Song of the Bell*, 152-154; removal to Weimar, 154; *Maria Stuart*, 156-158; visit to Dresden and Leipzig, 162; management of theatre, 162, 163; Kotzebue, 164; title of *von*, 165; *Bride of Messina*, 165; visit of Madame de Staël, 169; *William Tell*, 171-177; visit to Berlin, 177, 178; last visit to Jena, 179; *Demetrius*, 180-184; Spring of 1805, 185; death, 186; aristocratic temperament, 187; physical peculiarities, 188; family life, 189, 190; cheerfulness, 191; attempt to estimate his works and influence, 192-197.

Schlegel, 75, 106, 112

Schleswig Holstein Augustenburg, Prince of, 85, 86

INDEX. 203

Shelley, 40, 48
Staël, Madame de, saying about Schiller, 59; on *Maria Stuart*, 157; on the use of chorus, 167; visit to Weimar, 169-171
Stein, Frau von, 78
Stolberg, 108, 112

T.

Tell, begun, 169; completed, 171; general characteristics, 172, 173; scenery, 174; character of Tell, 175; death of Gessler, 176; fifth act, 177
Thalia, the Rhineland, 45, 52, 76, 90
Thirty Years' War, the History of, 79, 81, 83, 86
Turandot, 163

V.

Voltaire, 162, 163

W.

Wallenstein, composed, 127, 128; divisions, 129; the *Camp*, 130; Capuchin's sermon, 133-136; *Piccolomini*, 136-139; Max and Thekla, 139-142; Wallenstein's character and fate, 142-150; effect of the drama, 149
Weimar, Karl August, Grand-Duke of, early patronage of Schiller, 45; encouragement of Jena University, 75; bestows pension on Schiller, 78, 178
Weimar, 60, 61, 154, 192
Wieland, 61, 71, 112
Wolf, 113
Wolzogen, Frau von, Schiller's patroness, 24, 25; her son Wilhelm, 64
Wolzogen, Karoline von, Schiller's sister-in-law, 64, biography of Schiller, 67; friendship with Schiller, 78; marriage with Wolzogen, 107; account of Schiller's illness, 179-185
Würtemberg, Karl Eugen, Duke of, his part in the Seven Years' War, 12; his Court at Ludwigsburg, 13, 14; change in his character, 16; his Military Academy, 16-18; forbids Schiller to write, 22; indifference to Schiller's return, 95; death, 96

X.

Xenia, The, 109-114

BIBLIOGRAPHY.

BY

JOHN P. ANDERSON

(British Museum).

I. WORKS.
II. DRAMATIC WORKS.
III. HISTORICAL WORKS.
IV. LETTERS.
V. MISCELLANEOUS.
VI. POETICAL WORKS.
VII. TALES.
VIII. ESSAYS.
IX. SELECTIONS.
X. APPENDIX—
Biography, Criticism, etc.
Songs, etc., set to Music.
Magazine Articles.
XI. CHRONOLOGICAL LIST OF WORKS.

[*The Compiler has found it impracticable to give more than the first edition of the separate works in the original. All the English translations known to him have, however, been included.*]

I. WORKS.

Friedrich von Schiller's sämmtliche Werke. (Nachrichten von Schiller's Leben [by C. G. Körner]). 12 Bde. Stuttgart und Tübingen, 1812-15, 8vo.

Friedrich von Schiller's sämmtliche Werke. 16 Bde. Wien, 1816, 8vo.

Friedrich von Schiller's sämmtliche Werke. Zweyte unveränderte Auflage. Stuttgart und Tübingen, 1818-19, 8vo.

Friedrich Schiller's sämmtliche Werke. Original-Ausgabe. 18 Bde. Wien und Stuttgart, 1819-20, 8vo.

Friedrich Schiller's sämmtliche Werke in einem Bande, etc. Stuttgart, 1828-30, 8vo.

Schiller's sämmtliche Werke in einem Bande. Mit dem Portrait des Dichters, einem Facsimile seiner Handschrift und einem Anhang. Stuttgart und Tübingen, 1834, 8vo.

BIBLIOGRAPHY.

Schiller's sämmtliche Werke. Mit Stahlstichen. 12 Bde. Stuttgart und Tübingen, 1835-36, 8vo.

Sämmtliche Werke. Neue Ausgabe mit Stahlstichen. 12 Bde. Stuttgart, 1838, 16mo.

Schiller's sämmtliche Werke. 12 Bde. Leipzig [1867-68], 16mo.
Forms part of "P. Reclam's billigste Classiker-Ausgaben."

Schiller's sämmtliche Schriften. Historisch-kritische Ausgabe. Im Verein mit A. Ellissen, R. Köhler, W. Müldemer, H. Oesterley, H. Sauppe und W. Vollmer von K. Goedeke. 15 Thl. Stuttgart, 1867-76, 8vo.

Schiller's sämmtliche Werke. 12 Bde. Brünn, 1868, 16mo.

Schiller's sämmtliche Werke. Kritische Ausgabe von H. Kurz. 9 Bde. Hildburghausen, 1868-70, 8vo.

Schiller's Werke. (Herausgegeben von H. Kurz. Illustrirte Cabinets-Ausgabe.) 6 Bde. Stuttgart [1869], 8vo.
Forms part of "Göpel's Illustrirte Classiker-Ausgaben."

Schiller's Werke. Vollständige Ausgabe in einem Bande mit Portrait, einem Tonbild nach W. Kaulbach, etc. Teschen, 1871, 8vo.

Schiller's Werke. Erste Illustrirte Ausgabe. Mit Einleitungen von G. Wendt. 12 Bde. Berlin, 1874, 8vo.

Schiller's Werke. Illustrirt von den ersten deutschen Künstlern. Herausgegeben von J. G. Fischer. Mit mehr als 700 Illustrationen. 4 Bde. Stuttgart, 1879, 8vo.

Schiller's sämmtliche Werke. Mit Einleituugen von K. Goedeke. Stuttgart, 1881, 8vo.

The Works of Frederick Schiller. Translated from the German by the Rev. A. J. W. Morrison. 4 vols. London, 1846-9, 8vo.
Forms part of "Bohn's Standard Library."

Complete Works. [Translated from the German by S. T. Coleridge, Baron Lytton, H. G. Bohn, J. Churchill, and others.] Edited, with careful revisions and new translations, by C. J. Hempel. 2 vols. Philadelphia, 1870, 8vo.

Nachlese zu Schiller's Werken, oder Sammluug der vorzüglichsten prosaischen und poetischen Arbeiten, welche Schiller's Strenge gegen sich selbst in seine Werke nicht aufgenommen. Tübingen und Wien, 1810, 8vo.

Supplement zu F. von Schiller's sämmtliche Werken. Enthaltend: I. F. von Schiller's Briefe an den Freiherrn H. von Dalberg. II. Demetrius, ein Trauerspiel. Nach dem hinterlassenen Entwurfe des Dichters bearbeitet von F. von Maltitz. Zweite Auflage. Carlsruhe und Baden, 1824, 16mo.

Schiller's und Goethe's Leben, nebst kritischer Würdigung ihrer Schriften. Supplement zu deren sämmtlichen Werken von Viana. 2 Bde. Dinkelsbühl [1826], 8vo.

F. von Schiller's sämmtliche Werke. Ergänzungs-Band. Poetische und prosaische Aufsätze, vor dieser noch in keiner Sammlung von Schiller's Werken abgedruckt, als zum ersten

Mahle gesammelt von J. L. Greiner. Original - Ausgabe. Grätz, 1829, 12mo.
Nachträge zu Schiller's sämmtlichen Werken. Gesammelt und herausgegeben von E. Boas. 3 Bde. Stuttgart, 1839-40, 16mo.
Schiller's sämmtliche Werke. Ergänzungsband. Enthaltend: Don Carlos nach dessen ursprünglichem Entwurfe, zusammengestellt mit dem beiden späteren Bearbeitungen. Hannover, 1840, 16mo.
Nachlese zu Schiller's Werken nebst Varientensammlung, herausgegeben von K. Hoffmeister. 4 Bde. Stuttgart und Tübingen, 1840, 41, 16mo.
Supplement zu Schiller's sämmtlichen Werken. Schiller's Briefe. Mit erläuternden Anmerkungen herausgegeben von H. Döring. 2 Bde. Altenburg [1855], 16mo.

II. DRAMATIC WORKS.

Theater von Schiller. 5 Bde. Tübingen, 1805, 8vo.
Schiller's dramatische Entwürfe zum erstenmal veröffentlicht durch Schiller's Tochter E. Freifrau von Gleichen-Russwurm. Stuttgart, 1867, 8vo.
Schiller's dramatische Meisterwerke. Mit beleuchtenden Einleitung und Schiller's Lebensgang von H. Viehoff. Stuttgart, 1869, 16mo.
Schiller's Theater. 8 Bde. Stuttgart, 1871, 16mo.

———

Die Braut von Messina, oder die feindlichen Brüder, ein Trauerspiel mit Chören [in five acts, and in verse]. Tübingen, 1803, 8mo.
——The Bride of Messina, from the German, by G. Irvine, Esq. London, 1837, 8vo.
——The Bride of Messina: a tragedy. Translated by A. Lodge. London, 1841, 8vo.
——The Bride of Messina. To which is prefixed an essay on the tragical chorus. Translated by A. Lodge. The third edition. With other poems. London, 1863, 8vo.
——The Bride of Messina. Translated from the German in English verse. By E. Allfrey. London, 1876, 8vo.
Demetrius, ein Trauerspiel. Nach dem hinterlassenen Entwurfe des Dichters bearbeitet von Franz von Maltitz. Karlsruhe, 1817, 12mo.
Dom Carlos, Infant von Spanien, Trauerspiel. Leipzig, 1787, 8vo.
——Don Carlos, translated from the German. By the translators of Fiesco (G. H. Noehden, J. Stoddard). London, 1798, 8vo.
——Don Carlos, a tragedy, translated from the German. Third edition. London, 1798, 8vo.
——Don Carlos, Infant of Spain. A tragedy in five acts. Translated from the German of Frederick Schiller. By Benjamin Thompson. London, 1801, 8vo.
Part of vol. v. of the "German Theatre."
——Don Carlos, a tragedy. Translated and rendered into verse from the German of Schiller, etc. London, 1822, 8vo.

Don Carlos.—Don Karlos, a dramatical poem from the German by J. W. Bruce. Mannheim, 1837, 12mo.
——Don Carlos. Translated into English heroic metre by J. Towler. Carlsruhe, 1843, 8vo.
——Don Carlos, translated by C. H. Cottrell. Barnet [printed], London, 1843, 8vo.
——Second edition. London, 1844, 8vo.
——Don Carlos. Translated by T. S. Egan. London, 1867, 8vo.
——Don Carlos. Translated into English blank verse by A. Wood. Edinburgh, 1873, 8vo.
Die Huldigung der Künste. Stuttgart, 1804, 8vo.
——Schiller's Homage of the Arts, with miscellaneous pieces from Rückert, Freiligrath, and other German poets. [Translated.] By C. T. Brooks. New York [1846], 8vo.
Die Jungfrau von Orleans. Eine romantische Tragödie [in five acts and in verse]. Berlin, 1802, 12mo.
——The Maid of Orleans. Translated by J. E. Drinkwater. London, 1835, 8vo.
Privately printed.
——The Maid of Orleans. With a prologue. Translated by Egestorff. London, 1836, 8vo.
One of a series called "Egestorff's German Classics."
——The Maid of Orleans from the German. By N. J. Lucas. Bremen [printed], London [1841], 8vo.
——The Maid of Orleans, and other poems; translated from the German by E. S. and F. J. Turner. London, 1842, 12mo.

Die Jungfrau von Orleans.— The Maid of Orleans, and other poems. [Translated.] By W. Peter, etc. Cambridge [U.S.], 1843, 12mo.
——Selections from the Dramas of Goethe and Schiller, translated, with introductory remarks, by Anna Swanwick. London, 1843, 8vo.
Contains the "Maid of Orleans."
——The Maid of Orleans. Translated [by H. Thompson]. London [1845], 12mo.
Part of "Burns's Fireside Library."
——Specimens of Swedish and German Poetry, translated by J. E. D. Bethune. Part I. Poems of Esaias Tegner. Part II. Schiller's Maid of Orleans. London, 1848, 8vo.
——The Maid of Orleans: a romantic tragedy Rendered into English by L. Filmore. [With a prefatory note by E. G.] London [1882], 8vo.
Kabale und Liebe. Ein bürgerliches Trauerspiel in fünf Aufzügen [and in prose]. Mannheim, 1784, 8vo.
——Cabal and Love, a tragedy. Translated from the German of F. Schiller. [In five acts and in prose.] London, 1795, 8vo.
——Cabal and Love, a tragedy. Translated from the German, etc. London and Leipzic, 1796, 8vo.
——Second edition. London, 1797, 8vo.
——The Minister. Translated from the German [of the "Kabale und Liebe"] of Schiller, by M. G. Lewis. Second edition. London, 1798, 8vo.
——The Harper's Daughter, or Love and Ambition, a tragedy,

in five acts [and in prose]. Translated from the German [of the "Kabale uud Liebe"] of Schiller by M. G. Lewis, and now published with considerable alterations. Philadelphia, 1813, 16mo.

——Cabal and Love. Translated from the German, by T. C. Wilkinson. London, 1884, 8vo.

Macbeth, ein Trauerspiel von Shakespear. Zur Vorstellung auf dem Hoftheater zu Weimar eingerichtet von Schiller. Tübingen, 1801, 8vo.

Maria Stuart, ein Trauerspiel [in five acts and in verse]. Tübingen, 1801, 8vo.

——Mary Stuart, translated by J. C. M [ellish]. London, 1801, 8vo.

——Mary Stuart, a tragedy [in five acts and in verse]. The Maid of Orleans, a tragedy [in five acts and in verse]. From the German. With a life of the author by the Rev. H. Salvin, M.B. London, 1824, 8vo.

——Mary Stuart, a tragedy from the German of Schiller. London, 1838, 8vo.

——Mary Stuart. From the German of Schiller. [By Anne Trelawney.] Devonport, 1838, 8vo.

——Mary Stuart, from the German of Schiller. With other versions of some of his best poems. By W. Peter. Heidelberg, 1841, 8vo.

——Maria Stuarda, tragedia di cinque atti di F. Schiller. Versione Italiana di A. Maffei. Mary Stuart. Translated from the Italian version of A. Maffei by T. Williams. *Ital.* and *Eng.* London, 1856, 8vo.

Maria Stuart, ein Trauerspiel.— Plays by Frances Anne Kemble. An English tragedy; a play, iu five acts; Mary Stuart, translated from the German of Schiller, etc. London, 1863, 8vo.

——Mary Stuart, a tragedy. Translated by L. White. [With the original text.] London, 1882, 8vo.

Der Neffe als Onkel. Lustspiel in drei Aufzügen. Aus dem Französische des Picard. Stuttgart, 1808, 8vo.

——The Nephew as Uncle. A comedy in three acts [and in prose]. Translated from the German by G. S. Harris. Leipzig, 1856, 8vo.

——The Nephew as Uncle. A comedy in three acts, translated by T. C. Wilkinson. Ipswich [1882], 8vo.

Der Parasit, oder die Kunst sein Glück zu machen. Ein Lustspiel [in five acts and in prose] nach dem Französischen [of L. B. Picard]. Tübingen, 1806, 8vo.

——The Parasite, or the art to make one's fortune. A comedy [translated by Schiller from the French of L. B. Picard] in five acts, translated from the German of F. von Schiller, by F. Simpson. Leipzig, 1856, 8vo.

——The Parasite, a comedy imitated from the French by Schiller, and translated into English by J. S. S. Rothwell. Munich, 1859, 8vo.

Phädra. Trauerspiel von Racine. Uebersetzt von Schiller. Tübingen, 1805, 12mo.

Die Räuber. Ein Schauspiel. Frankfurt und Leipzig, 1781, 8vo.

Die Räuber.—The Robbers. A tragedy, translated from the German [by A .F. Tytler, Lord Woodhouselee]. London, 1792, 8vo.

——Second edition, corrected and improved. London, 1795, 8vo.

——Fourth edition, corrected and improved. London, 1800, 8vo.

——The Robbers, a tragedy in five acts. Translated and altered from the German, as it was performed at Brandenburgh House Theatre, 1798. London, 1799, 8vo.

——The Robbers, translated by the Rev. W. Render. London, 1799, 8vo.

——The Robbers, a tragedy in five acts. Translated from the German of Frederick Schiller. By Benjamin Thompson. London, 1800, 8vo.

Part of vol. v. of the "German Theatre."

Turandot, Prinzessin von China. Ein tragicomisches Mährchen nach Gozzi von Schiller. Tübingen, 1802, 8vo.

——Turandot, Princess of China, a tragi-comic drama [from the Italian of C. Gozzi], from the German of Schiller, with considerable alterations, by A. T. Gurney. Frankfort o. M., 1836, 8vo.

Die Verschwörung des Fiesko zu Genua. Ein republikanisches Trauerspiel von Friedrich Schiller. Mannheim, 1783, 8vo.

——Fiesco ; or, the Genoese Conspiracy, by G. H. N[oehden] and J. S[toddart]. London, 1796, 8vo.

——Fiesko, or the Conspiracy of Genoa. Translated from the German of Schiller [by Sir G. C. D'Aguilar]. Dublin, 1832, 8vo.

——Fiesco, or the Conspiracy of Genoa, a tragedy. Translated from the German. In five acts. London, 1841, 8vo.

——Fiesco, or the Revolt of Genoa ; an historical play in five acts. Altered from Schiller. London, 1850, 8vo.

Wallenstein, ein dramatisches Gedicht. (Wallenstein's Lager. Die Piccolomini, in fünf Aufzügen. Wallenstein's Tod, ein Trauerspiel in fünf Aufzügen). 2 Thle. Tübingen, 1800, 8vo.

——Wallenstein ; a dramatic poem. From the German [by G. Moir]. 2 vols. Edinburgh, 1827, 8vo.

——Wallenstein ; a drama done into English verse [with an introduction] by J. A. W. Hunter. London, 1885, 8vo.

——Wallenstein. Translated by C. G. N. Lockhart. London, 1887, 8vo.

——Wallenstein's Camp [translated] ; and original poems [by Lord F. L. Gower]. London, 1830, 8vo.

——Wallenstein's Camp, translated by E. Thornton. Frankfort-on-the-Main, 1854, 16mo.

——Wallenstein's Lager. In das Englische übersetzt von T. Wirgmann. Wallenstein's Camp. Translated into English verse by T. Wirgmann. Germ. and Eng. London, 1871, 8vo.

——The Piccolomini. Translated from the German of Friedrich Schiller by S. T. Coleridge. London, 1800, 8vo.

——The Piccolomini ; or, the first part of Wallenstein, etc. The

Death of Wallenstein. Translated from the German of Schiller. (Pp. 111-392 of S. T. Coleridge's "Select Poetical Works.") London, 1852, 12mo.
——Schiller's Tragedies : The Piccolomini ; and the Death of Wallenstein. Translated from the German by S. T. Coleridge. London, 1853, 8vo.
Vol. 1. Poetry, of the "Universal Library."
——The Piccolomini. Translated from the German. By W. R. Walkington. London, 1862, 8vo.
——The Tragedies of Schiller. The Piccolomini and Wallenstein. Translated by S. T. Coleridge. London, 1866, 8vo.
In "Masterpieces of Foreign Literature."
——The Death of Wallenstein. Translated by S. T. Coleridge. London, 1800, 8vo.
Wilhelm Tell. Schauspiel [in five acts and in verse]. Tübingen, 1804, 12mo.
——William Tell, a drama. Translated from the German of Friedrich Schiller. London, 1825, 8vo.
——William Tell, a play. Translated from the German, with notes. London, 1829, 8vo.
——William Tell. Translated by R. Talbot. London, 1829, 8vo.
——William Tell. A dramatic poem, translated. By T. C. Banfield. London, 1831, 8vo.
——William Tell, an historical play, from the German of Schiller, with notes and illustrations by W. Peter. Heidelberg, 1839, 8vo.
——Second edition. Luzern, 1867, 8vo.

Wilhelm Tell.—William Tell. From the German. London, 1845, 12mo.
Part of "Burns' Fireside Library."
——Schiller's William Tell. Translated into English verse. [By J. Cartwright.] London, 1869, 8vo.
——Schiller's William Tell. Translated into English verse. With an introductory essay. By D. C. Campbell. London, 1878, 8vo.
——Wilhelm Tell. A drama. Translated into English verse by E. Massie, etc. *Germ.* and *English.* Oxford, 1878, 8vo.
——Wilhelm Tell. A drama in five acts. Translated into English blank verse by Tarkári. London, 1879, 8vo.

III. HISTORICAL WORKS.

The Historical Works of Frederick Schiller. From the German, by George Moir. 2 vols. Edinburgh, 1828, 8vo.
Vols. 18-19 of "Constable's Miscellany."

Geschichte der merkwürdigsten Rebellionen und Verschwörungen aus den mittlern und neuern Zeiten. Bearbeitet von verschiedenen Verfassern, gesammelt und herausgegeben von Friedrich Schiller. Bd. 1. Leipzig, 1788, 8vo.
No more published.
Geschichte des Abfalls der Vereinigten Niederlande von der Spanischen Regierung. (Der Niederländische Revolution-

skrieg im 16ten und 17ten Jahrhundert; als Forsetzung der Schillerschen Geschichte von K. Curths.) 4 Thle. Leipzig, 1788-1810, 8vo.

——History of the Rise and Progress of the Belgian Republic. From the German of Friedrich Schiller, by T. Horne. London, 1807, 12mo.

——The History of the Defection of the United Netherlands from the Spanish Empire. Translated by E. B. Eastwick. Frankfort-on-the-Main, 1844, 12mo.

Friedrich Schiller's Geschichte des dreissigjährigen Kriegs. 2 Thle. Leipzig, 1791-93, 8vo.
   Appeared originally with the title "Historischer Calender für Damen auf die Jahre, 1791-93."

——The History of the Thirty Years' War in Germany. Translated by Captain Blaquiere, etc. [With preface by C. M. Wieland.] 2 vols. London, 1799, 8vo.

——The History of the Thirty Years' War in Germany. Translated by J. M. Duncan. 2 vols. London, 1828, 8vo.

Geschichte von Württemberg bis zum Jahr 1740 von Friedrich von Schiller. [Founded on lectures by Schott.] Zum ersten Male im Druck herausgegeben, etc. Stuttgart, 1859, 16mo.

Was heisst und zu welchem Ende studiert man Universalgeschichte. Eine akademische Autrittsrede. Zweite Auflage. Jena, 1789, 8vo.

IV. LETTERS.

Friedrich Schiller's Briefe an den Freiherrn H. von Dalberg in den Jahren 1781 bis 1785. [With a preface by M. Marx.] Carlsruhe und Baden, 1819, 8vo.

Briefwechsel zwischen Schiller und Goethe in den Jahren 1794 bis 1805. [Edited by the latter.] 6 Thle. Stuttgart und Tübingen, 1828, 1829, 8vo.

Correspondence between Schiller and Goethe, from 1794 to 1805, translated by G. H. Calvert. Vol. 1. New York [printed] and London, 1845, 12mo.

Correspondence between Schiller and Goethe, from 1794 to 1805. Translated from the third edition of the German, with notes. By L. D. Schmitz. 2 vols. London, 1877-79, 8vo.
   Part of "Bohn's Standard Library."

Schiller's Leben, verfasst aus Erinnerungen der Familie, seinen eignen Briefe und den Nachrichten seines Freundes Körner. (Von Karoline von Wolzogen.) 2 Thle. Stuttgart, 1830, 8vo.

Briefwechsel zwischen Schiller und W. von Humboldt. Mit einer Vorerinnerung über Schiller und den Gang seiner Geistesentwicklung von W. von Humboldt. Stuttgart und Tübingen, 1830, 8vo.

Friedrich von Schiller's Auserlesene Briefe in den Jahren 1781-1805. Herausgegeben von H. Doering. Zeitz, 1834, 8vo.

Biographie des Doctor F. W. von Hoven . . . und einem Anhang von 18 Briefen Friedrich Schiller's. Nürnberg, 1840, 8vo.

Andenken an Bartholomäus Fischenich. Meist aus Briefen Friedrichs von Schiller und

Charlottens von Schiller. Von Dr. H. Hennes. Stuttgart und Tübingen, 1841, 8vo.

Ungedruckte Briefe von Schiller, Goethe, und Wieland. Herausgegeben vom Justizrath Bitkow. Breslau, 1845, 8vo.

Briefe Schiller's und Goethe's an A. W. Schlegel, aus den Jahren 1795 bis 1801, und 1797 bis 1824, nebst einem Briefe Schlegels an Schiller. Leipzig, 1846, 8vo.

Schiller's und Fichte's Briefwechsel, aus dem Nachlasse des Erstern mit einem einleitenden Vorworte herausgegeben von J. H. Fichte. Berlin, 1847, 8vo.

Schiller's Briefwechsel mit Körner. Von 1784 bis zum Tode Schiller's. 4 Thle. Berlin, 1847, 8vo.

Correspondence of Schiller with Körner. Comprising sketches and anecdotes of Goethe, the Schlegels, Wieland, and other contemporaries. With biographical sketches and notes, by L. Simpson. 3 vols. London, 1849, 12mo.

Schiller in Briefen und Gesprächen. Sammlung der brieflichen und mündlichen Bemerkungen und Betrachtungen Schiller's über Werke und Erscheinungen der Wissenschaft und Kunst, des Lebens und der Menschenseele. Supplement zu den Werken des Dichters. Berlin, 1853, 8vo.

Schiller's Selbstcharakteristik nach des Dichters Briefen seit seinem achtzehnten Lebensjahre bis zum letzten, entworfen von Dr. H. Doering. Stuttgart, 1853, 8vo.

Schiller's Briefe. Mit geschichtlichen Erläuterungen, etc. 2 Bde. Berlin, 1854-57, 16mo.

Aus Weimars Glanzzeit. Ungedruckte Briefe von und über Goethe und Schiller, herausgeben von A. Diezmann. Leipzig, 1855, 8vo.

Schiller und Lotte. 1788, 1789. [Correspondence, edited by his daughter, E. von Gleichen Russwurm, assisted by J. H. Hennes.] Stuttgart und Augsburg, 1856, 8vo.

Schiller und Lotte. 1788-1805. Zweite, den ganzen Briefwechsel umfassende Ausgabe, bearbeitet von W. Fielitz. 3 Bücher. Stuttgart, 1879, 8vo.

Aus Herder's Nachlass. Ungedruckte Briefe von Herder und dessen Gattin, Goethe, Schiller, etc. 3 Bde. Frankfurt a. M., 1856-7, 8vo.

Briefe von Goethe, Schiller, Wieland, Kant, Böttiger, Dyk und Falk an Karl Morgenstern, herausgegeben von F. Sintenis. Dorpat, 1875, 8vo.

Schiller's Briefwechsel mit dem Herzog Friedrich Christian von Schleswig-Holstein-Augustenburg. Eingeleitet und herausgegeben von F. Max Müller. Berlin, 1875, 8vo.

Schiller's Briefwechsel mit seiner Schwester Christophine und seinem Schwager Reinwald. Herausgegeben von W. von Maltzahn. Leipzig, 1875, 8vo.

Geschäftsbriefe Schiller's Gesamwelt, erläutert und herausgegeben von K. Goedeke. Leipzig, 1875, 8vo.

Briefwechsel zwischen Schiller und Cotta. Herausgegeben

von W. Vollmer. Stuttgart, 1876, 8vo.
Ungedrucktes, von Albert Cohn. [Contains a number of the letters of Schiller]. Berlin, 1878, 8vo.
Schiller's ausgewählte Briefe. Selected and edited with an introduction and commentary by Pauline Buchheim. New York, 1886, 8vo.

V. MISCELLANEOUS.

Anthologie auf das Jahr [edited by Y., *i.e.*, J.C. F. von Schiller]. Tobolsko [Stuttgart], 1782, 8vo.
Allgemeine Sammlung historicher Memoires vom zwölften Jahrhundert bis auf die neuesten Zeiten durch mehrere Verfasser übersetzt, mit den nöthigen Anmerkungen versehen, und jedesmal mit einer universalhistorischen Uebersicht begleitet, herausgeben von Friedrich Schiller. (Erste Abtheilung, vierter Band, herausgegeben von Friedrich Schiller und K. L. Woltmann. Zum Schluss besorgt von H. E. G. Paulus.) 2 Abtheil. Jena, 1790-1806, 8vo.
Abtheil i. is in 4, and Abtheil ii. in 29 Bd.
Thalia. Herausgegeben von Schiller. 3 Bde. Leipzig, 1786-91, 8vo.
[Continued as]
Neue Thalia. Herausgegeben von Schiller. 4 Bde. Leipzig, 1792-93, 8vo.
Historischer Calender für Damen für das Jahre 1791-93, von Friedrich Schiller. Leipzig [1791-93], 12mo.
Die Horen, eine Monatsschrift herausgegeben von Schiller. 12 Bde. Tübingen, 1795-97, 8vo.
Museu Almanach für das Jahr 1796 (-1800). Herausgegeben von Schiller. Neustrelitz, Tübingen [1795-99], 12mo.
Journal für deutsche Frauen, von deutschen Frauen geschrieben. Besorgt von Wieland, Schiller, Rochlitz, und Seume. 2 Jahrg. in 6 Bde. Leipzig, 1805-6, 8vo.

VI. POETICAL WORKS.

Gedichte. 2 Thle. Leipzig, 1800-3, 8vo.
Lyrical Ballads from the German of Schiller; containing the "Song of the Bell," and other minor poems. By the translator of "Mary Stuart." Devonport, 1838, 12mo.
Select Minor Poems, translated from the German of Goethe and Schiller. With notes by John S. Dwight. Boston [U.S.], 1839, 8vo.
Vol. iii. of Ripley's "Specimens of Foreign Standard Literature."
The Minor Poems of Schiller of the second and third periods, with a few of those of earlier date, translated for the most parts into the same metres with the original by J. H. Merivale. London, 1844, 8vo.
Poems and Ballads, translated by Sir E. B. Lytton. With a brief sketch of Schiller's life. 2 vols. Edinburgh and London, 1844, 8vo.
——Second edition. Edinburgh and London, 1852, 8vo.
Schiller (Poems and Ballads) and Horace (Odes and Epodes).

Translated by Lord Lytton. London, 1875, 8vo.
  One of a collective series of Lord Lytton's works, entitled "The Knebworth Edition."
Schiller and Horace, translated by the Right Hon. Lord Lytton. London [1887], 8vo.
  Poems and Ballads of Schiller, pp. 15-276.
Schiller's Poems and Ballads, translated by Edward, Lord Lytton. With an introduction by Henry Morley. London, 1887, 8vo.
  Vol. 51 of "Morley's Universal Library."
The Poems and Ballads of Schiller. Translated by Sir Edward Bulwer Lytton. (*Chandos Classics.*) London, 1887, 8vo.
Favorite Poems. Translated by Sir E. Lytton Bulwer. Boston [U.S.], 1877, 16mo.
The Poems of Schiller complete. Attempted in English by E. A. Bowring. London, 1851, 8vo.
——Second edition. London, 1874, 8vo.
  Part of "Bohn's Standard Library."
Specimens of Friedrich Schiller's Minor Poems. [Translated by S. R.] London, 1867, 8vo.
Schiller's Minor Poems and Ballads, with notes by Arthur P. Vernon. London [1887], 8vo.
Original Poems. Translations of Demetrius, part of the Bride of Messina, etc. By Charles Hodge. Munich, 1836, 8vo.
Collection of Select Pieces of Poetry, containing the Lay of the Bell and some minor poems of Frederick Schiller, etc. By George Ph. Maurer. Darmstadt, 1840, 8vo.

Ballads of Schiller. No. 1. The Diver: with notes. Rev. Frederick K. Harford. London, 1878, 4to.
Elegie auf den frühzeitigen Tod Johann Christian Weckelius von seinen Freunden. Stuttgart, 1781, fol.
Fridolin, or the road to the iron foundry, a ballad. By Friedrich Schiller, with a translation by J. P. Collier, illustrated with eight engravings in outline by H. Moses from the designs of Retsch. London, 1824, 4to.
——Another edition. London [1875], obl. 4to.
The Fight with the Dragon. A Romance [Der Kampf mit dem Drachen], with a translation by J. P. Collier, with sixteen engravings in outline by H. Moses, from the designs of Retsch. *Germ.* and *Eng.* London, 1825, 4to.
——The Fight with the Dragon. A romance translated [from the German] by J. P. Collier. Illustrated with engravings in outline by H. Moses from the designs by Retzsch. London [1875], obl. 4to.
Die Künstler. Ein didactisches Gedicht. Erläutert von F. Friedemann. Leipzig, 1875, 8vo.
Schiller's Lied an die Freude. Illustrationen gezeichnet von L. Löffler. Zweite Auflage, vermehrt durch Erläuterungen von Dr. M. Schasler. Leipzig [1859], fol.
The Song of the Bell. Translated by W. H. Furness, with illustrations by A. L. Mayer,

and with vignettes by R. Seitz. London [1800], fol.

——Faust: a drama, by Goethe, and Schiller's Song of the Bell, translated by Lord Francis Leveson Gower. London, 1823, 8vo.

——The Song of the Bell. Translated from the German. With the original. London, 1827, 8vo.

——The Song of the Bell, translated from the German. Bath, 1828, 12mo.

——The Song of the Bell, and other poems. From the German of Goethe, Schiller, Bürger, etc. Translated by John J. Campbell. Edinburgh, 1836, 8vo.

——Schiller's Song of the Bell. Translated for the Boston Academy of Music. By S. A. Eliot. Boston [U.S.], 1837, 8vo.

——The Song of the Bell; and other poems; translated from the German [by M. M.—*i.e.*, M. Montagu. With notes]. London, 1839, 8vo.

——Das Lied von der Glocke. With English translation, by T. J. Arnold. *Germ.* and *Eng.* London, 1842, 8vo.

——A Selection of German Poetry, etc. By George Egestorff. No. 1 containing Schiller's Lay of the Bell. *Germ.* and *Eng.* London, 1844, 8vo.

——Schiller's Song of the Bell; with an English literal translation, and a vocabulary to every page. By H. A. Meeson. *Germ.* and *Eng.* London, 1846, 16mo.

——Verse Translations from the German: including Bürger's Lenore, Schiller's Song of the Bell, and other poems. London, 1847, 8vo.

——The Song of the Bell, translated from the German of Schiller. By R. H. A. Martin. Exeter, 1849, 8vo.

——Das Lied von der Glocke. The Song of the Bell, by Schiller. With a translation [into English verse] by J. H. Merivale. *Germ.* and *Eng.* London and Edinburgh, 1856, 8vo.

——Another edition. London, 1869, 8vo.

——The Song of the Bell. Translated from Schiller. Dublin, 1857, 12mo.

——Das Lied von der Glocke, mit kurzer biographischer Einleitung zur Erinnerung an die hundertjährige Geburtstags-Feier Friedrich Schiller's. The Lay of the Bell, with a biographical sketch of its author, Friedrich Schiller. *Germ.* and *Eng.* London, 1859, 8vo.

——Schiller's Lay of the Bell. Translated by the Right Hon. Sir E. B. Lytton, Bart. With illustrations drawn on wood by T. Scott, and engraved by J. D. Cooper after designs by M. Retzsch. London, 1865 [1864], obl. 4to.

——Schiller's Song of the Bell; translated by W. H. Furness. With illustrations by C. Jaeger and A. Mueller. London [1874], 4to.

——The Song of the Bell, the Gods of Greece, and other ballads. Paraphrased from Schiller by A. Mills. London, 1876, 8vo.

——Schiller's Lay of the Bell,

translated [in verse] from the German, by G. B. Holmes. London, 1877, 8vo.
——The Lay of the Bell, and Fridolin. Translated by Sir E. Bulwer Lytton. Illustrated. Boston [Mass.], 1877, 16mo.
——The Lay of the Bell and other Ballads. Translated into English metre, by A. Wood. *Germ.* and *Eng.* Edinburgh, 1879, 8vo.
The Song of the Bell. Translated by W. H. Furness. With illustrations by Meyer, etc. Munich [1880], fol.
——Schiller's Song of the Bell [translated by W. H. Furness], with illustrations by A. L. Mayer and E. H. Garrett. Boston; Cambridge [Mass., printed], 1883, 8vo.
Resignation, nebst Witschel's Antwort auf dieselbe. Kreuznach [183—], 12mo.
The Knight of Toggenburg [Ritter Toggenburg]. Translated from the German of Schiller [by W. W.—*i.e.*, W. Whewell]. Shelford, 1842, 4to.
Nine leaves, printed on one side only.
The Walk [Der Spaziergang] translated [by Sir J. W. Herschel] in the original metre from the German. *Germ.* and *Eng.* [London ? 1844 ?] obl. 8vo.
Privately printed.
Der Venuswagen. [A poem.] [Stuttgard, 1782], 8vo.

VII. TALES.

The German Novelists: Tales selected from ancient and modern authors, etc. By Thomas Roscoe. 4 vols. London, 1826, 8vo.
Vol. iii. contains several of Schiller's tales.
Der Geisterseher. Eine Geschichte aus dem Memoires des Grafen von O**. Leipzig, 1789, 8vo.
——The Ghost-Seer ; or, Apparitionist. An interesting fragment, found among the papers of Count O****, from the German of Schiller. [Translated by D. Boileau.] London, 1795, 8vo.
——The Armenian ; or, the Ghost Seer. A history founded on fact. Translated from the German by W. Render. 4 vols. London, 1800, 12mo.
——The Ghost-Seer ! From the German of Schiller. 2 vols. London, 1831, 8vo.
Part of vols. ix-x. of the *Standard Novels*.
The Criminal become so from lost [sic] of honour. Translated from the original German [Der Verbrecher aus verlorener Ehre] of Friedrich Schiller by L. Wapler. Augsburg, 1825, 8vo.
Privately printed.
——The Dishonoured Irreclaimable. (Pp. 139-175 of "Tales from the German," by Richard Holcraft. London, 1826, 8vo.
——The Criminal, in consequence of Lost Reputation. A true history. Translated for the "Romancist" from the German of Frederick Schiller. London, 1841, 8vo.
Part of vol. iii. of the *Romancist*, edited by William Hazlitt.
——The Criminal from Lost Honour. (In *Tales from the German.*) Translated by John Oxenford and C. A. Feiling. London, 1844, 8vo.

VIII. ESSAYS.

Kleinere prosaische Schriften aus mehrern Zeitschriften vom Verfasser selbst gesammelt und verbessert. 4 Thle. Leipzig, 1792-1802, 8vo.

The Philosophical and Æsthetic Letters and Essays of Schiller. Translated, with an introduction, by J. Weiss. London, 1845, 8vo.
Part of the "Catholic Series."
——Another edition. Boston, 1845, 8vo.

Essays, æsthetical and philosophical; including the dissertation on the "Connexion between the Animal and Spiritual in Man." Newly translated from the German. London, 1875, 8vo.
Part of "Bohn's Standard Library."

Schiller's erste bis jetzt unbekannte Jugendschrift. Amberg, 1839, 8vo.

Versuch über den Zusammenhang der thierischen Natur des Menschen mit seiner Geistigen. Stuttgard, [1780], 4to.

IX. SELECTIONS.

Geist aus Friedrich Schiller's Werken, gesammelt von C. F. Michaelis. Nebst einer Vorrede über Schiller's Genie und Verdienst, etc. 2 Abth. Leipzig. 1805-6, 8vo.

Beantwortung aus der Religion aufgeworfener Fragen durch Sprüche aus Schiller's Werken. Crefeld, 1824, 12mo.

Schiller's politisches Vermächtniss. Ein Seitenstück zu Börne's Briefen aus Paris. [Extracts, with a preface by J. C., *i.e.*, Joachim Campe?] Hamburg, 1832, 12mo.

Schiller Ansichten des Dichters über Gott, Natur und Menschheit aus seinen Gedichten und Dramen zusammengestellt von F. d'Hargues. Berlin, 1859, 12mo.

Aphorismen aus Schiller's Werken. Ausgewählt und herausgegeben von N. Bausch. Ulm, 1865, 8vo.

Guilt; or, the Gipsey's Prophecy; a tragedy by A. Müllner; followed by Schiller's "Ideal" and "The Cranes of Ibycus," translated from the original German. By W. E. Frye. London, 1819, 8vo.

Specimens of the German Lyric Poets: consisting of translations in verse, from the works of Bürger, Goethe, Klopstock, Schiller, etc. Second edition. London, 1823, 8vo.

Translations from the German; and original poems. By Lord Francis Leveson Gower. London, 1824, 8vo.
Schiller, pp. 3-50.

Specimens of the German Lyric Poets. London, 1828, 8vo.
Contains a number of translations from Schiller.

Employment. [Poems translated by F. Page from the German of Schiller and Goethe.] Bath, 1828, 8vo.

The Poets and Poetry of Europe. By Henry Wadsworth Longfellow. Philadelphia, 1845, 8vo.
Schiller, pp. 305-316.

German Ballads, Songs, etc., comprising translations from

Schiller, Uhland, etc. London [1845], 8vo.
Forms part of Burns's "Fireside Library."
English Hexameter Translations from Schiller [by J. F. W. H., *i.e.*, Sir J. F. W. Herschel, W. W., *i.e.*, W. Whewell, and J. C. H., *i.e.*, J. C. Hoare], Göthe [by the same W. W. and J. C. H.], Homer, etc. London, 1847, obl. 8vo.
Metrical Translations from the German of Goethe, Schiller, Uhland, Heine, and others, by a German Lady. Hamburg, 1852, 8vo.
Echoes; or, Leisure Hours with the German Poets. By A. C. Kendrick. Rochester [U.S.], 1855, 8vo.
Schiller, pp. 3-55.
Flowers from Fatherland [*i.e.*, poems by G. A. Bürger, J. C. F. Schiller, etc.] transplanted into English soil. By J. P. Trotter, A. M. Adam, and G. Coltman. [Edited by A. M. Adam.] Edinburgh, 1850, 8vo.

X. APPENDIX.

BIOGRAPHY, CRITICISM, ETC.

[*This list consists of the English literature on Schiller, the German title being given only in those cases where the work has been translated into English.*]

Bach, Edmund.—The Poems of Schiller explained, etc. London, 1840, 8vo.
Bancroft, G.—Literary and Historical Miscellanies. New York, 1855, 8vo.
The Age of Schiller and Goethe, p. 167, etc.
Barnett, Morris. — Power and Principle, a drama in three acts (founded upon von Schiller's "Kabale und Liebe.") London [1851], 12mo.
Part of vol. ii. of "Lacy's Acting Edition of Plays."
Boyesen, Hjalmar H. — Goethe and Schiller; their lives and works, etc. New York, 1879, 8vo.
Carlyle, Thomas. — The Life of Friedrich Schiller. Comprehending an examination of his works. London, 1825, 8vo.
——Second edition. London, 1845, 8vo.
De Quincey, Thomas.—The Works of Thomas de Quincey, etc. Second edition. 16 vols. Edinburgh, 1862-71, 8vo.
Schiller, vol. xv., pp. 181-204.
Düntzer, Heinrich. — Schiller's Leben von Heinrich Düntzer. Leipzig, 1881, 8vo.
——The Life of Schiller. By Heinrich Düntzer. Translated by Percy E. Pinkerton. London, 1883, 8vo.
Ellet, Elizabeth F.—The Characters of Schiller. Boston [U.S.], 1839, 8vo.
Encyclopædia Britannica.—Encyclopædia Britannica. London, 1886, 4to.
Schiller, by James Sime, vol. xxi.
Förster, Erwin.—Schiller-Gallerie. Nach Originalzeichnungen von W. v. Kaulbach, Prof. C. Jäger and Prof. A. Müller. Photographische Album-Ausgabe von E. Förster. München [1867], 4to.
——Schiller Gallerie. [Photographs.] From the original drawings of W. Kaulbach, C. Jäger, etc. With explanatory text by E. Förster. Leipzig, [1873], 4to.

―Another edition. Munich [1874], fol.

Gandy, Edward.—Lorenzo, the Outcast Son. A tragic drama. Founded on the Robbers of Frederic Schiller. London, 1823, 8vo.

Gostwick, Joseph.—The Spirit of German Poetry; a series of translations from the German poets. By Joseph Gostwick. London, 1845, 8vo.
Schiller, pp. 59-82.

—German Poets. A series of memoirs and translations. London [1875], 8vo.
Schiller, pp. 155-178.

—German Culture and Christianity. London, 1882, 8vo.
Schiller, pp. 318-346.

Gostwick, Joseph, and Harrison, Robert.—Outlines of German Literature. Second edition. London, 1883, 8vo.
Schiller, pp. 304-342.

Grimm, Herman.—Essays. *Germ.* Hanover, 1859, 8vo.
Schiller und Goethe, pp. 291-353.

—Goethe. 2 Bde. Berlin, 1877, 8vo.
References to Schiller, Bd. ii., pp. 107-178.

—The Life and Times of Goethe. Translated by Sarah H. Adams. Boston [U.S.], 1880, 8vo.
Schiller, pp. 357-363; Schiller and Goethe—their estrangement, pp. 364-382; Goethe's Union with Schiller,—Schiller's Wife, pp. 383-403; Goethe and Schiller in Weimar, pp. 404-419; Schiller and Goethe, pp. 410-441.

Hedge, Frederic H. — Prose Writers of Germany. New edition. Philadelphia [1872], 8vo.
Schiller, pp. 365-382.

—Hours with German Classics. Boston [U.S.], 1886, 8vo.
Schiller, pp. 344-395.

Holman, J. G.—The Red-Cross Knights. A play founded on the Robbers of Schiller. By J. G. Holman. London, 1799, 8vo.

Jefferys, Charles.—An English version of Verdi's tragic opera, Louisa Miller. Written and adapted by Charles Jefferys. [Founded on "Kabale und Liebe."] Melbourne [1871], 8vo.

McCarthy, Justin. — "Con Amore;" or, critical chapters. London, 1868, 8vo.
Friedrich Schiller, pp. 77-147.

Metcalfe, Rev. Frederick—History of German Literature. London, 1858, 8vo.
Schiller, pp. 453-467.

Nevinson, Henry.—A sketch of Herder and his times. London, 1884, 8vo.
References to Schiller.

Niblett, Alfred N. — Schiller; dramatist, historian, and poet. A centenary lecture, etc. London and Edinburgh, 1860, 8vo.

Pagel, L.—Doctor Faustus of the popular legend, Marlowe, the Puppet Play, Goethe and Lenau, treated historically and critically. A parallel between Goethe and Schiller, etc. Liverpool [1883], 8vo.

Palleske, Emil.—Schiller's Leben und Werke. 2 Bde. Berlin, 1858, 8vo.

—Schiller's Life and Works. Translated by Lady Wallace. 2 vols. London, 1860, 8vo.

Rudloff, F. W. — Shakespeare, Schiller, and Goethe, relatively considered. An essay. Brighton, 1848, 8vo.

Scherer, Wilhelm. — Geschichte der Deutschen Litteratur. Berlin, 1883, 8vo.
Schiller und Goethe, pp. 552-581; Schiller, pp. 581-613.

Scherer, Wilhelm.—A History of German Literature. Translated by Mrs. F. C. Conybeare. Edited by F. Max Müller. 2 vols. Oxford, 1886, 8vo.
<small>Schiller and Goethe, vol. ii., pp. 170-190; Schiller, pp. 199-231.</small>

Schiller, Friedrich.—Lorenzo, the Outcast Son. A tragic drama [in three acts and in verse], founded on the Robbers of F. Schiller. London, 1823, 8vo.

——I Briganti. The Brigands, a serious opera, in three acts. [Founded on "Die Räuber."] *Ital.* and *Eng.* London, 1836, 8vo.

Sime, James.—Schiller. London, 1882, 8vo.
<small>One of the "Foreign Classics for English Readers," edited by Mrs. Oliphant.</small>

Solling, Gustav.—Diutinska, an historical and critical Survey of the Literature of Germany, etc. London, 1863, 8vo.
<small>Schiller, pp. 289-365.</small>

Taylor, Bayard.—Studies in German Literature. London, 1879, 8vo.
<small>Schiller, pp. 266-303.</small>

Taylor, William, *of Norwich.*— Historic Survey of German Poetry, interspersed with various translations. 3 vols. London, 1828, 8vo.
<small>Life and Works of Schiller, vol. iii., pp. 167-241.</small>

Thimm, Franz.—The Literature of Germany, etc. London, 1886, 8vo.
<small>Schiller, pp. 130-147.</small>

Werner, Friedrich.—The Characteristics of Schiller's Dramas, with preliminary notes on the poet's life. London, 1859, 12mo.

Wilson, H. Schütze.—Count Egmont; as depicted in painting, poetry, and history, by Gallait, Goethe, and Schiller. London, 1873, 8vo.

SONGS, ETC., SET TO MUSIC.

"Die Braut von Messina." Tragic Opera, by J. H. Bonawitz, 1874.

"Don Carlos." Grand Opera, by Verdi, 1867.

"Luisa Miller" [Opera founded on *Kabale und Liebe*]; by Verdi, 1859.

Schiller's Lyrische Gedichte in Musik gesetzt; by J. H. Reichardt, 1810.

Das Lied von der Glocke von Schiller, in Musik gesetzt; von A. Romberg, 1810.

Die Glocke. Cantate, by C. Haslinger, 1845.

Hochzeit der Thetis. Grosse Cantate, by J. C. G. Loewe, 1840.

Nanie, Cantata; by J. Brahms, 1882.

To the Sons of Art. Cantata by Mendelssohn, 1869.

Beatrice. Scene aus Schiller's "Braut von Messina," by F. von Holstein, 1877.

Demetrius. Scene der Marfa aus Schiller's Drama, by J. Joachim, 1878.

Zwölf Schiller-Lieder, by L. Gaulke and E. Rohde, 1859.

Lieder von Schiller, by G. Weber, 1820.

Sechs Gedichte von Schiller, by C. F. Curschmann, 1840.

Sechs deutsche Lieder von Schiller, by C. F. Rungenhagen, 1810.

Sechs deutsche Lieder von Schiller, by C. J. P. Schulz, 1810.

V. Gedichte von Schiller, by C. F. Curschmann, 1830.
Drei Lieder von Luther und Schiller, by C. Reinthaler, 1860.
Three German Songs, poetry by Schiller; by H. Wylde, 1845.

"Ach! aus dieses Thales Gründen" (Callcott's *Vocal Gems of Germany*, Vol. 3), 1844; by A. Romberg, 1820 ["Ah! from out this vale's recesses"]; by F. Schubert, 1850.
"An der Quelle sass der Knabe;" by H. Proch (Les concerts de Société, No. 16), 1845; H. von Siegroth, 1865.
"Auch das Schöne muss sterben," by J. Brahms, 1882.
"Ehret die Frauen," by J. F. H. Dalberg (Zwölf Lieder, No. 1), 1799.
"Der Eichwald brauset," by W. Haeser (Neun deutsche Lieder, Op. 34, No. 5), 1854; J. Holter (Vier Gesänge, No. 3), 1881; J. Reinberger (Wache Träume, No. 7), 1872; M. V. White, 1884.
"Es donnern die Hohen," by W. Rust (Zwei vierstimmige Lieder, Op. 30, No. 2), 1875.
"Es steht ein gross geräumig Haus," by H. C. Deacon, 1878.
"From this valley's lowly plain," by W. L. Phillips, 1866; H. Smart (Cramer's Glees, No. 36), 1874.
"Freude, schöne Götter-Funken," by Beethoven (Choral Symphony, No. 9), 1824; Baron Dalberg (Zwölf Lieder, No. 3), 1799.
"Der Gang nach den Eisenhammer," by R. Randegger, 1873; B. A. Weber, 1810.

"Die Glocke," by F. F. Hurka, 1805.
"Hear I the creaking gate unclose," by W. H. Phipps, 1850.
"Heil'ge Nacht, du sinkest nieder," by R. Emmerich (Fünf Gesänge, Op. 42, No. 5), 1874.
"King Francis the combat awaited," by C. F. Zelter, 1805.
"Die Künstler," by E. Lassen, 1875.
"Leben athme die bildende Kunst," by C. F. Rungenhagen (Sechs deutsche Lieder), 1810.
"Lebt wohl ihr Berge," by F. M. Leslie, 1863; Lady E. Tollemache, 1866.
"Das Lied von der Glocke," by M. Bruch, 1879; F. F. Hurka, 1802; A. Romberg, 1810; C. Stoer (Tonbilder für Orchester), 1872.
"Lay of the Bell," by A. Romberg, 1854.
"Die Macht des Gesanges," by A. Romberg, 1810, 1815, 1875.
"Nenie," by H. Goetz, 1876.
"Nestor jetzt der alte Zecher," by O. Ladendorff, 1886.
"Nimmer, das glaubt mir, erschienen die Götter," by M. Bruch, 1874.
"Noch in meines Lebens Lenze," 1878.
"Schiller's Ode an die Freude," by T. von Ferguson, 1830.
"O'er Heidelberg's old castle," by R. F. Harvey, 1856.
"Oh! that I could wing my way," by Miss Davis, 1866.
"Ritter treue Schwesterliebe," by J. R. Zumsteeg, 1805.
"Das Siegesfest," by B. Scholz, 1884.
"Siehe wie schwebenden Schritts," by J. F. Borschitzky, 1859.

"Der Taucher," by F. A. Kaune, 1815.
"Trommeln und Pfeifen Krieg' rischer Klang," by E. Lassen (Sechs Lieder, Op. 61, No. 6), 1877.
"Von Perlen baut sich eine Brücke," by H. C. Deacon, 1878.
"Vor seinem Löwengarten," by R. Felsz, 1884; D. Fischers, 1882.
"Weit in nebelgrauer Ferne," by H. Schnaubelt (Vier zweistimmige Gesänge, Op. 23, No. 1), 1869.
"Willkommen du O Wonne der Natur," by J. F. Radoux (Vingt Mélodies, No. 10), 1875.
"Willkommen schöner Jüngling," by M. Zenger, 1864.
"Will sich Hektor ewig von mir wenden?" by G. C. Grosheim, 1795.
"Willst du nicht das Lammlein hüten?" by J. F. Reichardt, 1845.
"Wohl perlet im Glase der purpurne Wein," by M. Bruch (Fünf Lieder, Op. 38, No. 5), 1875.
"Die Worte des Glaubens als." Cantate bearbeitet, by A. Schmitt, 1855.

MAGAZINE ARTICLES, ETC.

Schiller, Friedrich. Fraser's Magazine, by T. Carlyle, vol. 3, 1831, pp. 127-152.— Dublin University Magazine, vol. 7, 1836, pp. 3-23.—North British Review, by J. F. Gordon, vol. 3, 1845, pp. 154-165.— Sharpe's London Magazine, vol. 2, 1846, pp. 17-21, 52, 53.— Bentley's Miscellany (portrait),

Schiller, Friedrich. by C. Whitehead, vol. 25, 1849, pp. 193-196.—Godey's Magazine, vol. 43, 1852, pp. 267-269. —Eclectic Magazine (from the Biographical Magazine), vol. 28, 1853, pp. 313-326.—Tait's Edinburgh Magazine, vol. 24, 2nd ser., 1857, pp. 167-173.— London Quarterly, vol. 14, 1860, pp. 109-148.—Methodist Quarterly, vol. 46, 1864, pp. 242-256. — Argosy, by Alice King, vol. 12, 1871, pp. 276-282.—Blackwood's Edinburgh Magazine, vol. 114, 1873, pp. 183-206; same article, Littell's Living Age, vol. 118, pp. 707-724, and Eclectic Magazine, vol. 18 N.S. pp. 513-530.
——and Alfieri. Southern Literary Messenger, by Mrs. E. F. Ellet, vol. 2, 1836, pp. 702-714.
——and Duke of Schleswig-Holstein, Correspondence. Macmillan's Magazine, by F. M. Müller, vol. 34, 1876, pp. 368-384; same article, Littell's Living Age, vol. 131, pp. 23-35.
——and Goethe. Monthly Review, vol. 10 N.S., 1829, pp. 525-534.—Edinburgh Review, vol. 53, 1831, pp. 82-104.
—— ——Goethe and Madame de Staël. Fraser's Magazine, vol. 5, 1832, pp. 171-176.
—— ——and Goethe, Characteristics of. Dublin University Magazine, vol. 87, 1876, pp. 684-688.
—— ——and Goethe, Correspondence of. Foreign Quarterly Review, vol. 7, 1831, pp. 180-183.
—— ——and Goethe, Friendship of. New Englander, by W. H. Wynn, vol. 32, 1873, pp. 718-737.

Schiller, Friedrich.
—— ——*and Goethe, Poems of.* Boston Quarterly Review, vol. 2, 1839, pp. 187-205.
——*and his Plays.* Hogg's Instructor, vol. 6 N.S., 1856, pp. 35-40.
——*and his Times.* New Monthly Magazine, vol. 117, 1859, pp. 446-452.
——*Ballads.* London Society, vol. 3, 1863, pp. 273-277.
——*Bride of Messina.* Edinburgh Review, vol. 65, 1837, pp. 239-251.
——*Characters of.* Hesperian, vol. 3, 1839, pp. 208-211.
——*Complaint of Ceres;* translated. Blackwood's Edinburgh Magazine, vol. 4, 1818, pp, 161-164.
——*Correspondence with Körner.* Southern Literary Messenger, vol. 15, 1849, pp. 109-111.
——*Cranes of Ibycus;* translated. Blackwood's Edinburgh Magazine, vol. 38, 1835, pp. 302, 303. Sharpe's London Journal, by George Bullen, vol. 10, 1849, pp. 14, 15.
——*Diver;* translated. Fraser's Magazine, by E. Webbe, vol. 15, 1837, pp. 229-231.—Dublin University Magazine, vol. 5, 183', pp. 590-593. — Blackwood's Edinburgh Magazine, vol. 25, 1829, pp. 778-781.
——*Don Carlos.* New Monthly Magazine, vol. 4 N.S., 1822, pp. 56-62.
——*English and American Translations.* Dublin University Magazine, vol. 24, 1844, pp. 379-399.
——*Ethical Studies of.* Journal of Speculative Philosophy, vol. 12, 1878, pp. 373-392.

Schiller, Friedrich.
——*Fiesko.* Blackwood's Edinburgh Magazine, by R. P. Gillies, vol. 16, 1824, pp. 194-202.
——*Fight with the Dragon;* translated. Blackwood's Edinburgh Magazine, vol. 38, 1835, pp. 649-652.
——*Flight from Stuttgart.* Foreign Quarterly Review, vol. 22, 1839, pp. 348-355.
——*Hero and Leander;* translated. Dublin University Magazine, by J. Anster, vol. 23, 1844, pp. 452-457.
——*Homage of the Fine Arts;* translated. Catholic World, by A. F. Hewit, vol. 31, 1880, pp. 299-307.
——*Journal.* Penn Monthly Magazine, vol. 5, 1874, pp. 878-881.
——*Last Moments of.* People's Journal, vol. 2, 1847, pp. 21, 22.
——*Less Translatable Poems of.* Dublin University Magazine, vol. 12, 1838, pp. 46-64.
——*Life of.* Eclectic Review, vol. 24 N.S., 1825, pp. 248-259. —North American Review, vol. 39, 1834, pp. 1-30.—Christian Examiner, by F. H. Hedge, vol. 16, 1834, pp. 365-392.—Edinburgh Review, vol. 73, 1841, pp. 151-188.—Dublin Review, vol. 11, 1841, pp. 477-505.— Southern Literary Messenger, by J. T. Lomax, vol. 7, 1841, pp. 162-164.— Foreign Quarterly Review, vol. 30, 1843, pp. 281-315.—Eclectic Magazine, vol. 5, 1845, pp. 467-474; vol. 8, pp. 433-444.
——*Life and Writings.* London Magazine, vol. 8, 1823, pp. 381-400; vol. 9, pp. 37-59; vol. 10,

BIBLIOGRAPHY. xxi

Schiller, Friedrich.
pp. 16-25, 149-163, 259-269.—
North American Review, by
A. H. Everett, vol. 16, 1823,
pp. 397-425.
—— *Maid of Orleans.* Blackwood's Edinburgh Magazine,
vol. 56, 1844, pp. 216-227.—
Eclectic Magazine, vol. 10, 1847,
pp. 357-375.
—— *Mary Stuart.* Knickerbocker, vol. 9, 1837, pp. 433-446.—Monthly Review, vol. 3
N.S., 1843, pp. 182-198.
—— *Minor Poems.* North American Review, by G. Bancroft,
vol. 17, 1823, pp. 268-287.—
Dublin University Magazine,
vol. 5, 1835, pp. 39-57.
—— *Murderess*; translation. Blackwood's Edinburgh Magazine, vol.
3, 1818, p. 418.
—— *Nannette.* Galaxy, by Mary
A. E. Wager, vol. 20, 1875, pp.
675-684.
—— *Poems.* Eclectic Review, vol.
16 N.S., 1844, pp. 177-189.—
Irish Quarterly, vol. 2, 1852,
pp. 461-493.
—— *Poems*; translated. Blackwood's Edinburgh Magazine, by
E. Lytton Bulwer, vol. 52, 1842,
pp. 285-298, 751-766; vol. 53,
pp. 166-180, 626-639; vol. 54,
pp. 139-152.
—— *Poems, by Bulwer.* Monthly
Review, vol. 2 N.S., 1844, pp.
47-60.
—— *Remains, Story of.* Macmillan's Magazine, by A. Hamilton, vol. 8, 1863, pp. 302-310;
same article, Littell's Living
Age, vol. 78, pp. 522-528.
—— *Ring of Polycrates.* Blackwood's Edinburgh Magazine,
vol. 43, 1838, pp. 684-685.
—— *Shakespeare and Æschylus.*

Schiller, Friedrich.
Blackwood's Edinburgh Magazine, vol. 69, 1851, pp. 641-660.
—— *Song of the Bell.* Dublin
University Magazine, vol. 5,
1835, pp. 141-151.—Christian
Examiner, by N. L. Frothingham, vol. 22, 1837, pp. 235-245.
—Tait's Edinburgh Magazine,
vol. 11 N.S., 1844, pp. 82-84.
—Democratic Review, vol. 16
N.S., 1845, pp. 215-222.
—— —— *Song of the Bell;* Furness's translation. Knickerbocker, vol. 37, 1851, pp. 357-361.
—— —— *Song of the Bell;* translated. New Monthly Magazine,
vol. 58, 1840, pp. 129-139.
—— *Sir Toggenburg;* translated.
Blackwood's Edinburgh Magazine, vol. 25, 1829, pp. 80, 81.
—— *Sport of Fortune;* translated.
Blackwood's Edinburgh Magazine, vol. 8, 1820, pp. 375-381.
—— *Translation of Macbeth.* Dublin University Magazine, vol.
84, 1874, pp. 498-505.
—— *Translations from.* Dublin
University Magazine, vol. 3,
1834, pp. 43-45, 113-116.—
Fraser's Magazine, vol. 44,
1851, pp. 165-171.
—— *Wallenstein.* Monthly Review, vol. 5 N.S., 1827, pp.
483-488; vol. 14 N.S., 1830,
pp. 570-590.—London Magazine, vol. 7 N.S., 1827, pp.
460-466. — Retrospective Review, vol. 1, 2nd Series, 1827,
pp. 40-55.—Dublin University
Magazine, vol. 8, 1836, pp. 721-737.—Dublin University Magazine, vol. 9, 1837, pp. 33-46.—
Westminster Review, vol. 53,
1850, pp. 349-365.
—— —— *Wallenstein;* translated
by Coleridge. Blackwood's

BIBLIOGRAPHY.

Schiller, Friedrich.
Edinburgh Magazine, vol. 14, 1823, pp. 377-396.
——*Weimar under, and Goethe.* Contemporary Review, by H. S. Wilson, vol. 29, 1877, pp. 271-288 ; same article, Littell's Living Age, vol. 132, pp. 550-560.
——*Wilhelm Tell.* Blackwood's Edinburgh Magazine, vol. 17, 1825, pp. 299-318.—Monthly

Schiller, Friedrich.
Review, vol. 108 N.S., 1825, pp. 344-352 ; vol. 12 N.S., 1829, pp. 505-513.—American Monthly Magazine, vol. 3 N.S., 1837, pp. 587-600.—Christian Examiner, by J. S. Dwight, vol. 25, 1839, pp. 385-391.
—— ——*Peter's Translation of Wilhelm Tell.* Monthly Review, vol. 3 N.S., 1840, pp. 181-195.

XI. CHRONOLOGICAL LIST OF WORKS.

Versuch über den Zusammenhang der thierischen Natur des Menschen mit seiner Geistigen . . 1780	Kleinere prossaische Schriften . . 1792-1802
Die Räuber . . . 1781	Die Horen . . 1795-97
Der Venuswagen . . 1782	Musen Almanach . 1795-99
Die Verschwörung des Fiesko zu Genua . . 1783	Wallenstein . . . 1800
Kabale und Liebe . . 1784	Gedichte . . 1800-3
Thalia [continued as] Neue Thalia . . . 1786-93	Maria Stuart . . . 1801
Dom Carlos . . . 1787	Macbeth (*Trans.*) . . 1801
Geschichte des Abfalls der vereinigten Niederlande von der Spanischen Regierung . . 1788-1810	Turandot (*Trans.*) . . 1802
	Die Jungfrau von Orleans 1802
	Die Braut von Messina . 1803
	Wilhelm Tell . . . 1804
Geschichte der merkwurdigsten Rebellion aus dem mittlern und neuern Zeiten . . . 1788	Die Huldigung der Künste 1804
	Phädra (*Trans.*) . . 1805
	Journal für deutsche Frauen 1805-6
Der Geisterseher . . 1789	Der Parasit (*Trans.*) . . 1806
Was heisst und zu welchem Ende studiert man Universal-geschichte . . 1789	Der Neffe als Onkel (*Trans.*) 1808
	Demetrius . . . 1817
	Geschichte von Württemberg bis zum Jahr 1740 . 1859
Historischer Calender für Damen für das Jahre 1791-1793	Briefe an H. von Dalberg . 1819
Geschichte des dreissigjahrigen Kriegs . 1791-93	Briefwechsel zwischen Schiller und Goethe 1828, 29
	Briefwechsel zwischen Schiller und W. von Humboldt . . . 1830

BIBLIOGRAPHY. xxiii

Auserlesene Briefe in den Jahren 1781-1805	1834	Geschäftsbriefe Schiller's	1875
Ungedruckte Briefe von Schiller, Goethe, und Wieland	1845	Briefwechsel mit dem Herzog Friedrich Christian von Schleswig-Holstein-Augestenburg	1875
Briefe Schiller und Goethes an A. W. Schlegel	1846	Briefwechsel mit seiner Schwester Christophine	
Briefwechsel mit Körner	1847	und seinen Schwager Reinhald	1875
Schiller's und Fichte's Briefwechsel	1847	Briefwechsel zwischen	
Schiller's Briefe	1854-57	Schiller und Cotta	1876
Schiller und Lotte, 1788, 1789	1856	Schiller und Lotte. 1788-1805	1879

Printed by WALTER SCOTT, *Felling, Newcastle-on-Tyne.*

www.ingramcontent.com/pod-product-compliance
Lightning Source LLC
Chambersburg PA
CBHW031814230426
43669CB00009B/1139